Collecting Movie Posters

Collecting Movie Posters

An Illustrated Reference Guide to Movie Art—Posters, Press Kits, and Lobby Cards

EDWIN E. POOLE and SUSAN T. POOLE

McFarland & Company, Inc., Publishers
Jefferson, North Carolina, and London

British Library Cataloguing-in-Publication data are available

Library of Congress Cataloguing-in-Publication Data

Poole, Edwin E., 1948–
    Collecting movie posters : an illustrated reference guide to
movie art—posters, press kits, and lobby cards / Edwin E. Poole
and Susan T. Poole.
        p.   cm.
    Includes bibliographical references and index.
    ISBN 0-7864-0169-9 (sewn softcover : 50# alkaline paper) ∞
    1. Film posters—Collectors and collecting.   I. Poole, Susan T.,
1953–   . II. Title.
PN1995.9.P5P58   1997
791. 43'075—dc21   96-48836
                                                        CIP

Manufactured in the United States of America

McFarland & Company, Inc., Publishers
  Box 611, Jefferson, North Carolina 28640

Table of Contents

Acknowledgments

This project would not have been possible without the help and support of the following individuals who assisted in the gathering and compiling of the information found in this book: Leith Adams of Warner Bros. Studio in Los Angeles, California; Applied Graphics of Los Angeles, California; Richard Arceneaux, private poster collector/dealer in New Orleans, Louisiana; Crowell Havens Beech, poster dealer and professional poster restorer in Belvedere Island, California; Herb Bennett, Manager of Cox Cable in New Orleans, Louisiana; Mr. Benton of Benton Card Company in Benson, North Carolina; Joseph Berger, Librarian of the Enoch Pratt Free Library in Baltimore, Maryland; Tony Calvert, poster dealer in Tyler, Texas; Bill Cobb, retired owner of Theatre Poster Exchange in New Orleans, Louisiana; John Hazelton, poster dealer in Mineola, New York; Jeff Kilian of Kilian Enterprises in Wichita, Kansas; John Kisch, private poster collector/dealer and author of *A Separate Cinema* and the *Data Base Price Guides*, Hyde Park, New York; Joe McNair, private poster collector in New Orleans, Louisiana; Man Pham, photographer in New Orleans, Louisiana; Tim Rich of Gone Hollywood; Tarra Gin Di, Queensland, Australia; Joe Van Rogers, private poster collector in Brooklyn, New York; A.J. Roquevort, Jr., of New Orleans, Louisiana; Jim Sherraden, Manager of Hatch Show Prints of Nashville, Tennessee; and David R. Smith, Director of Archives at Disney Studios in Burbank, California.

The authors also wish to acknowledge the love and support of our children Sarah and David "Buddy" Poole, and family June Trog, June and George Armstrong, who have personally endured throughout the years the trials and tribulations associated with our "passion for posters," and whose help (that priceless DZ card) was invaluable to the completion of this book.

Preface

When we first began collecting movie posters around 1985 we had no idea that it would eventually lead to a personal career—but it has. Movie poster collecting has evolved from a hobby shared by a select few to a fast rising industry reaching into mainstream America. We have gotten caught up in this movement—and we love it. We went from collector/hobbyist to dealer in a relatively short period of time, and we have witnessed some rather drastic changes in the way collectors look at the movie poster industry.

In the beginning, we encountered a world comprised of a very elite, tight circle of individuals with a language all their own. These movie poster collectors represented a small number of individuals who shared a rare but common bond. These pioneer collectors completely controlled the industry, thus establishing poster values for the titles that were of particular interest to them. The years have seen an increase in the number of collectors, loosening the control of the older collectors and creating a more liberal market. However, it is not always easy for a new collector to feel at ease.

We made many mistakes and met a few individuals lacking in conscience when we began our hobby. We soon learned, however, that the more we knew, the less chance we had of making mistakes. Unfortunately, there was nothing on the market available in the way of reference materials, and we gained our knowledge through trial and error. Because we want to see this industry grow and appeal to new collectors, we decided to write this book.

Before beginning this book, we spoke to a number of seasoned collectors to get their opinion on how we should approach our project. The comment we received most often from these veterans was, "Why is such a book needed?" Many of them do not see the need for any type of reference materials, feeling that the best way to learn is through experience. We, on the other hand, believe that a general knowledge of the industry can eliminate many of the more common mistakes made by many collectors, including those with some experience. Thus, we have written this book with would-be, newer and intermediate collectors in mind.

Because our intent is to reach across a wide spectrum of collectors, we have had to present the material in the broadest light possible. For example, to many veteran collectors, posters printed after the 1960s are undesirable, and thus uncollectible. In fact, they hold to a strict definition of movie art—that is, only posters that were actually sent to a theatre qualify as true movie poster collectibles. The newer breed of collectors, however, looks at the movie poster industry in much broader terms. For example, the age of a poster is not significant if it is a desirable title. Many of the posters for recent Walt Disney cartoon features will sell for prices much higher than those of posters thirty or forty years older.

Another trend in poster collecting is following the career of a particular individual. For these collectors, posters of any kind are considered collectible, including video and television. Other collectors look at special anniversary issues as collectible movie art, while their hard-line counterparts view these posters as merely commercial reproductions. In short, the emergence of a newer breed of movie poster collector has caused a departure from the once established definition of movie poster collector. As such, we have included in this book a wide range of subjects that relate to the current movie poster market, even though some items may not be considered as part of the "legitimate movie poster market" to some collectors.

Please note that the movie art industry is broad by its nature, and the materials that comprise it are as unique and individual as the movies they represent. As such, it is difficult to apply strict definitions and guidelines to its common terms. Many of the terms are subjective in nature, and therefore will differ in meaning from one collector to another. The areas of this book that address condition and grading are particularly subjective. We have, however, made every effort to provide the most commonly applied meaning for each term.

While every attempt has been made to provide complete and accurate definitions, errors and omissions may occur. This book was not written as a substitute for expert opinions; before any major purchases are made, consultation with a movie poster expert knowledgeable of the particular time period in question is highly recommended.

We hope that this book will be of some help to you while you discover the exciting world of movie art.

Introduction

When you're standing in the line at a theatre and you look over the poster that is displayed in the window that advertises the current feature, what do you see? Do you see a product created by some New York ad agency for the purpose of luring you (and your wallet) into a particular movie theatre, or do you view that poster in terms of its creativity, beauty and detail? Does that poster represent a cheap piece of advertising or a key to a future generation's understanding of our present-day society? When you come across a movie poster from a film from bygone years, do you wonder what it was that possessed someone to keep it, or do you suddenly experience the rush of wonderful memories of a movie you saw during happy, carefree times from your past? Do you see a worthless piece of paper or a valuable memento from movie history?

Most people view movie posters in the same light as do the movie studios that produce them—as an expensive form of expendable advertising materials to be used for a short period of time then thrown out with the trash. Certain others, however, see things a bit differently. This somewhat elite group of individuals (to which the authors proudly belong) view movie posters through the eyes and with the heart of one who possess a "collector's spirit"—those who perceive a deeper value in items that most view as valueless. Movie posters, while on the surface are merely advertising tools, present tangible reminders of the best and worst in film history. Movie art collectors, and those who are prospective candidates to become collectors, view movie posters with this "collector's spirit."

What Is Movie Art?

Remember the last time you were inside of a typical movie theatre. As you looked around at the walls in the lobby, you probably saw posters of the feature or features which were currently playing or which were coming soon. These posters may have been displayed in glass surrounded by marquee style lights. If you are a baby-boomer or older, you may even have seen some smaller "cards" or odd-sized posters lined along the walls of the lobby. You may also have passed a store on your way to the theatre and seen smaller versions of the "posters" in storefront windows. Younger readers may have noticed mini posters, stand-ups, counter displays or mobiles. You may have seen advertisements in the movie section of your newspaper. All of these items fall into the category of movie art.

Since posters and related movie art materials are used as advertising tools by major studios to lure prospective moviegoers to their particular films, they are designed specifically to get your attention and to promote the film in the greatest light. While the beauty and aesthetic value of posters vary from studio to studio, they all have one basic purpose—to promote box-office sales and to get you into their theatre.

Note: The movie posters and other advertising materials that are used by theatres should not be confused with posters that can be purchased from stores or discount chains. The posters found in retail outlets are printed on a commercial basis in large numbers and generally should not be taken into consideration when discussing collectible movie art. We will address the differences later on in this book.

Who Collects Movie Art?

Up until the 1970s, movie art collectors were relatively small in number and the members of this elitist group set the standards for the entire movie art industry. While the reasons for movie art collecting vary with each individual, most people believe that the first collectors did so strictly out of love and enjoyment of a movie, or a star, or the movie industry in general. It is hard to fathom that anyone could have foreseen that these materials, which were intended solely as disposable advertising materials, would some day be in such demand. But, for whatever reasons, these pioneers possessed the "collector's spirit" and saw the value of these posters as pieces of movie history.

As the years passed, more and more of these materials were destroyed, either intentionally or with age, and more and more collectors joined the ranks in an attempt to salvage these pieces of art. Today, there are literally thousands of serious collectors, and this number is expected to continue to climb. There are also a great deal of "not so serious" collectors who enjoy collecting their favorite movie materials, regardless of their value. Regardless of the underlying reason, movie poster collecting is on the verge of enjoying widespread appeal.

How Does Movie Art Compare with Other Collectibles?

There are literally thousands of items that can be classified as "collectibles." The more popular collectibles include baseball cards, football cards, comic books, stamps, and rarer items such as porcelain pieces, art, and the like. But these collectibles have several disadvantages. Because of the popularity of sports cards, they can be found in discount chains, neighborhood convenience stores and grocery stores. They are produced in such large numbers that rarity is practically nonexistent. Of course, there are the rarer baseball and football cards from earlier decades, but the prices on these cards are very costly, and it is very difficult for first-time collectors to get a good start.

The same holds true for comic books. Costs of old and rare comic books are high. The newer comic books are printed in such mass that their value as a collectible is diminished. Other collectibles are very costly and it is extremely hard for new collectors to get started. So how does movie art collecting differ? There are a number of reasons why movie art stands apart from all other collectibles.

- Popularity of Movies
- Not Made for Public Sale
- Works of Art
- Can Be Started with Little Money

Popularity of Movies

It is a safe assumption that most people, at some point in their life, have seen a motion picture. It is also safe to assume that everyone has seen at least one motion picture or one movie star or personality that he or she truly loved. The real truth is that millions of people have seen and see movies every day, and there are literally millions of movie fans worldwide.

Movie art collecting offers the avid movie fan an opportunity to possess something tangible from their favorite movie or star. They can own a piece of the movie, as the movie advertising items are as much a part of the whole movie process as are the script, the stars, the directors, and the cast. Through movie art collecting, movie fans can own and display some special limited quantity memento of their favorite motion picture.

It is a safe bet that the love affair between movies and the public will continue. And as more and more moviegoers discover movie art collecting, the more demand for these materials will grow. As the demand increases, value increases, thereby creating the possibility of turning a very enjoyable hobby into a future investment.

Not for Public Sale

As in any industry, advertising plays a key role in the movie-making business. There are literally hundreds of movies released every year, and the studios are vying for public interest in their particular projects. To assist the theatres in promoting the various releases, the movie studios produce and provide materials that are designed by their advertising departments to assist theatres in putting on a successful movie campaign. These materials are not released to the public. As such, they are printed in limited numbers—only enough to accommodate the local theatres. They are strictly advertising materials—meant to be discarded after the movie's run.

Of all the reasons why people collect movie art, none seems to compare to the very basic instinct in all of us that we would like to have something that most other people will never have. Because of the limited numbers produced; because of the number of them destroyed, either intentionally or through age; because they are not meant for public sale; and because they can only be acquired through limited avenues, movie art offers rarity in a world of mass production.

Note: For clarification purposes, we are addressing legitimate theatre advertising materials and not commercially produced posters and the like. The differences in the kinds of movie art are addressed in the reference section of this book.

Works of Art

Many of the advertising materials produced for motion pictures are truly "works of art." In fact, many studios contract with well-known artists to produce the artwork used in the advertising materials. Some of the better known artists of today are Amsel, Peak, Drew and the Hildebrandt brothers. Even the legendary Norman Rockwell has lent his talents to movie art.

Framed and mounted, some movie posters will compete aesthetically with any legitimate piece of art. Many favorites come from the sci-fi and horror categories which feature outstanding and sometimes breathtaking graphic artwork. Many posters from little known hits are true collector's items just because of their beauty. In many cases, posters from better known movies cannot compete with those of the genre known as "B" movies. Of course, this is understandable since producers of some of the better known movies do not have to overcome public uncertainty when they boast celebrity stars. The lesser known movies depend entirely on their advertising materials to make or break the movie. In any case, movie art offers an alternative to mainstream artwork at prices that are much more in line with the average person's budget.

Little Money Required

Since movie art collecting has existed in an elite circle of collectors, they have basically set the guidelines for determining a poster's value. In the past, the focus of these collectors has been on horror films from the 1930s and movie classics from the golden era (such as *Gone with the Wind*). As such, the prices of these posters have gone through the roof, while other films' posters from the same era have enjoyed only a fractional increase in value. Recently, movie art collectors have turned their attention to certain horror movies of the 1950s, causing prices on such notable films as *Forbidden Planet* and *The Day the Earth Stood Still* to skyrocket. The secret for those just entering the market is to take advantage of these "sleepers" now, before they become sought-after materials.

Posters of more currently released movies can have an almost instantaneous impact on collectors. *Star Wars* material is always wanted by collectors. *Blade Runner*, *E.T.* and a host of other movie favorites from the 1970s and 1980s have already moved to the level of "preferred collectibles." Walt Disney introduced a special numbered edition poster of the *Rocketeer* in 1990, which was produced in limited quantities. In 1991, Walt Disney released a special edition poster of *Beauty and the Beast*, the animated film. Less than one year after the poster's debut, it had already enjoyed an increase of over 500 percent in value.

Movie art collecting offers a wide selection of low, medium or high priced materials for the first time collectors. Whether you have lots or just a little to start your collection, there are excellent opportunities for all.

History of the Movies
and the Movie Poster

Although considered a relatively new medium to most, the movie industry has been in existence for over one hundred years. The movie poster, in all of its sizes and forms, has been an interesting feature of this industry since the very beginning. Volumes have been written about the history of the movie industry. However, there is little written information about the history of the movie poster. The following is a brief look into the history of the motion picture as it relates to the movie poster.

Early Movie Inventions

During the late 1800s, many inventors experimented with devices that would make pictures appear to move. The Belgian scientist, Joseph Plateau, invented the *phenakistoscope* in 1832. This device consisted of two disks a few inches apart on a rod. Plateau placed painted pictures of a person or thing on the edge of one of the disks, each picture being slightly advanced. The other disk had slots, so when both disks were rotated at the same speed, the pictures appeared to move as they came into the view of the slots.

There were a number of inventors throughout France, Great Britain and the United States attempting to create a means of projecting moving pictures. While no one really knows who actually first produced and projected a motion picture, several gentlemen are given the credit.

With the aid of transparent celluloid film developed by Hannibal W. Goodwin, and the photographic equipment manufactured by George Eastman, Thomas Edison and William Dickson began work on their invention, which they called the *kinetoscope*. The kinetoscope was a cabinet with about 50 feet of film on spools. While viewing through a peephole, patrons would turn a crank which made the spools move. This gave the appearance of moving pictures.

In 1894 Edison opened the Kinetoscope Parlor in New York, containing two rows of coin-operated kinetoscopes where patrons could view one to two minute moving picture shows. Kinetoscopes were soon found in London and Paris. While Edison considered moving pictures as a passing fad soon to fade, other inventors recognized the potential and began work on improving cameras and projection equipment.

Early Movie Exhibitions

While the United States was enjoying the new motion picture fad, French brothers Auguste and Louis Lumière were working on their own projection invention. On February 13, 1895, they patented their first projection machine, and on March 28, 1895, their first film, *Lunch Hour at the Lumière Factory* was shown to the Société d'Encouragement de l'Industrie Nationale. On December 28, 1895, in the Salon Indien of the Grand Cafe, 14 boulevard des Capucines, the Lumières presented the first short film to be projected on a screen publicly in front of an audience. The film was titled *L'Arrivée d'un train en gare*, and consisted of scenes of a train arriving at a station. Soon movies were being shown in all major cities throughout Europe.

Back in the United States, Edison continued his work on the kinetoscope. After adapting his device for projection capabilities, Edison presented his first public exhibition of motion pictures projected on a screen at Koster and Bial's Music Hall in New York City on April 23, 1896. The program consisted of a performance by a dancer, a prize fight and scenes of waves rolling on a beach. The first American cinema was Vitascope Hall, which opened on June 26, 1896, in New Orleans, Louisiana. The theatre had 400 seats and its program consisted of short scenic items.

The First Movie Posters

Soon public exhibitions were a regular happening, and exhibitors began to look at ways to compete with patrons. The earliest forms of movie advertising included the use of hand-painted crates and sandwich boards. But this crude form of advertising would soon be obsolete thanks to the artistic contributions of Frenchman Jules Cheret.

At the turn of the century, the world had a very high illiteracy rate. Posters, with their vibrant colors and pictures, and limited words, provided a means of advertising on a level that could be understood by the majority of the general public. Posters could be placed almost anywhere in the city and were widely used to promote a variety of products and services, including the early cinema.

Jules Cheret, considered in the advertising world as the father of the modern poster, is also credited with bringing the movie poster into existence. Through the use of the printing process known as stone lithography (which was invented around 1798), Cheret produced a lithograph for the 1890 short film program called *Projections Artistiques*. The lithograph showed a young lady holding a placard with the times of the shows. Cheret followed with his poster for Émile Reynaud's Théâtre Optique 1892 program called *Pantomines Lumineuses*.

The first posters used to advertise moving pictures portrayed an audience watching black and white images projected on a screen. These posters contained the name of the movie company, such as Edison or Lumière, and the name of the hall showing the program. They did not even mention the title of the program. The programs were five to ten minutes long and were changed about twice a week. Because the posters did not contain the titles, they could be used time and again.

In 1896, M. Auzolle designed the first poster for a specific film, actually containing scenes from the program, for Lumière's film entitled *L'Arroseur Arrosé*. This film is also generally considered the first movie with a fictitious plot. The film's plot involved a young boy who squeezed a gardener's hose, prompting the gardener to look into the hose to see what was stopping the water's flow. As the boy released the hose, the gardener was sprayed with water. The boy's prank resulted in a spanking.

The 1900s

The movies up to this point in time were nothing more than pictures of actual events, such as waves washing against a beach. While the initial motion pictures flourished, after a while the crowds began to grow bored, and the motion picture industry faced its first sense of doom. In 1899, Georges Méliès, a French magician, produced the first motion picture to tell an entire story. He filmed hundreds of fairy tales and science fiction stories. Other movie producers followed, and interest in motion pictures again began to flourish.

By 1900, motion pictures were enjoying enormous popularity throughout the United States and Europe. Motion pictures became popular attractions at amusement parks, music halls, traveling fairs and vaudeville theatres. The vaudeville style "stock poster" was soon gaining favor with the movie companies. One of the earliest of these was produced by the American Entertainment Company. It measured 28" × 42" and depicted an audience watching an on-screen brass band. The scene was possibly taken from one of Edison's early works.

Some of the other commonly used stock posters depicted ladies holding up a card which would give the show's program for the night. These stock posters could be reused by simply placing a new program on top of an older program.

In 1903, Edwin S. Porter, an American director, produced the first motion picture utilizing modern film techniques to tell a story. The film, *The Great Train Robbery*, was an eleven minute movie describing a train robbery and the pursuit and capture of the robbers. This movie was a tremendous hit, and this film's success led to the establishment of "nickelodeons," the forerunner to movie theatres.

Initially begun in 1905 by an ingenious Pittsburgh businessman, nickelodeons were stores which were converted into early theatres by simply adding chairs. These nickelodeons charged five cents and showed a variety of movies, accompanied by piano music. By 1907, there were approximately 5,000 nickelodeons throughout the United States, and the demand for new movies was continually growing.

By 1909, the number of companies producing movies was growing by leaps and bounds. Although Thomas Edison resented the fact that these newcomers were profiting from what he considered to be his invention, he decided that it would be best to join forces with the larger studios in an attempt to shut out the smaller ones. The major studios at the time, Biograph, Essanay, Kalem, Kleine, Lubin, Selig and Vitagraph, joined Edison to form the Motion Picture Patents Company. This group of studios also organized the General Film Company to distribute the studios' films to theatres.

One of the first steps made by this newly-formed cartel was to set standards for advertising materials. Although Edison had used Hennegan Show Print in Cincinnati for printing posters for his first films, the General Film Company contracted with A. B. See Lithograph Company of Cleveland to produce all the members' posters and ad materials.

The first standardized size of poster became known as the "one sheet," measuring 27" × 41". The one sheet was designed to be used in glass display cases inside and outside of movie theatres. The first such one sheets depicted the company identity, the film's title and plot. Each of the member companies had its own stock poster borders printed in either two or three colors. There was a white panel left in the center which would have the title and description of the movie's plot. In some cases, even the ending was printed. The posters sometimes included a photograph supplied by the movie's producing company.

Strict censorship standards were established by the General Film Company, and all member companies were required to meet these rigid standards. In most cases, the photographs were rather tame in nature, and usually showed the leading man and lady. The producing companies paid A. B. See for the posters and then sold them to the individual nickelodeons or movie houses for about fifteen cents each.

Since the A. B. See posters were subject to the scrutiny of the Patents Company, independent lithographers began printing generic posters showing scenes varying from romantic embraces to shootouts. These posters were popular with many theatre owners because they were considerably cheaper (about six cents), could be used over and over, and were more graphic and uncensored than the materials sanctioned by Edison's Patents Company.

The 1910s

Up to this point in film history, there were no "movie stars." Most of the actors in the early films chose to remain anonymous. It was to the benefit of all involved with early films to keep their movie's participants unknown. Legitimate state actors preferred to remain unknown, embarrassed that anyone would find out that they participated in this new medium. Movie producers were secure in knowing that they could control the medium as long as the movie participants remained unnamed.

By the year 1910, however, things began to change. As early as 1908, studios began receiving mail addressed to nameless actors. Movie producers, fearing that giving the identity of the stars would cause them to demand more money, continued to insist on anonymity. But the studios were soon faced with the reality that moviegoers wanted to know the names of the actors and actresses. This would become quite evident thanks to the stunt perpetrated on the industry by Carl Laemmle, owner of IMP studio.

Laemmle managed to steal one Florence Lawrence from a rival movie studio. To this point, Lawrence was known to her fans as the "Biograph Girl." In what could be considered one of the first publicity stunts pulled off by a movie studio, a rumor was started, purportedly by Laemmle himself, that the adored "Biograph Girl" was dead. In order to set the record straight, Laemmle published a full page ad in a St. Louis newspaper stating that he had "nailed a lie" and would be presenting Lawrence in St. Louis. When more people showed up to see Lawrence than had come to see then President Taft who was visiting St. Louis one week earlier, the studio owners had to acquiesce, and no longer would movie actors and actresses be kept anonymous.

It was at this point that producers recognized that the real selling tools were not the movies but the "stars" that graced their screens. Suddenly, posters had to be designed with consideration given to the stars and their pecking order. Posters now had to reflect the size and status of the "leading lady" and "leading man." Soon the public could recognize one's star status simply by looking at a movie poster. The size of the print and the placement were easy indicators as to just how big a particular star was. Movie contracts would now include clauses relating to the size and placement of names on the movie poster and other advertising materials. Actors and actresses had now become powers with which to be reckoned.

By the early 1910s, nickelodeons were being replaced by movie theatres. These theatres had more room to advertise their new films, which had now moved to two reels. To complement the one sheet, new advertising sizes and types were introduced by the Patents Company.

Lobby cards were smaller in size and were normally printed in sets of eight. The first of these cards were actually 8" × 10" black and white stills, which were printed in sepia or duotone and tinted by hand. They were later replaced with 11" × 14" color lobby card sets. These sets normally contained eight scenes from the movie which were normally displayed in series in the theatre lobby.

A larger sized paper was also being introduced at this time. Known as the "three sheet," it measured 41" × 81" and was so named because it was three times the size of a one sheet. An even larger size was introduced called the "six sheet." The six sheet, being six times the size of a one sheet, measured 81" × 81". These materials were created to be displayed in larger areas in and around the theatres.

Edison's Patents Company was dissolved through court litigation. The dissolution of this company had a direct effect on movie posters. No longer restricted by the censorship guidelines imposed by Edison's companies, A. B. See Lithographers could create more lavishly produced materials without any restriction. The movie companies could then distribute the posters and other materials through their own exchanges or could assign them to agencies who rented them. These posters could be reused time and again. The posters that were muslin-backed could be used almost indefinitely.

With more films on the market, competition heated up and movie studios widened their advertising boundaries to include areas outside of the movie theatre. With new roadways being built and the number of cars on these new roads, movie companies recognized that the highway's "open spaces" offered another advertising medium—the billboard. The "24 sheet," as it was known, measured 246" × 108", exactly 24 times the size of the one sheet. These billboards could be noticed at great distances, and studios utilized the talents of many recognized artists to design their 24 sheets.

In order to take advantage of the number of window, pole and wall spaces around a community, a new form of advertising paper was introduced. These new materials, called window cards, were printed on card stock and measured 14" × 22", with a wide top border which was used to print show times and dates. Window cards were purchased in bulk by the theatres and film exchanges, and were placed in retail and office windows, on poles, on walls—anywhere there was space.

With the increasing number of studio-owned theatre chains, movie studios would map out a full national advertising campaign. As part of this campaign, the studios would produce a series of press materials that could be used by the theatres and film exhibitors to promote a movie. These "press books," as they were most commonly called, were introduced around 1917. The "press books" would sometimes be a part of a "press kit," which, in addition to press information, would include special promotional ideas. These materials were also referred to by other names, most commonly "showman's manual" or "campaign book."

The 1920s

The early 1920s were considered the golden age of the silent movie. Grand movie palaces soon replaced the movie theatre, and the crude posters of old gave way to more splendid, artistically accomplished movie posters. Well known commercial artists were commissioned by many studios to design movie poster "portraits" of leading stars. Unfortunately, the American studios did not allow the artists to sign their posters, as commercial artists were allowed to do on European movie posters.

These new posters no longer depicted scenes—the posters were designed with portraits of the stars, the movie title and the stars' names. There was an occasional slogan or two, but the emphasis was now placed on the stars. Most of the studios had their advertising offices in New York, and this is where most of the posters originated from.

It was during this time that the National Screen Service (NSS) first made its appearance. The NSS began competing with the studios' lucrative business of creating and distributing "trailers." Trailers were the film clips of coming attractions that would be shown after a feature presentation—thus the term trailer. It would be two more decades before NSS would be a predominant factor in the movie paper industry.

By the mid–1920s, movie theatre owners and film exhibitors were provided with a full array of promotional materials for their use in advertising. Up to this point, most of the materials were printed and distributed by the studios. However, a number of independent "secondary" printers began issuing various forms of movie posters, giving theatres and film exhibitors an alternative to the studio-produced materials.

By the 1920s, a new printing process was developed. Known as photogelatin or heliotype, this new process was used primarily on smaller sized card stock items, such as lobby cards, inserts and window cards. Evolving from one color to three (yellow, pink and blue), this process was used for materials meant to be viewed closely. These items were not as effective when viewed from a distance. One sheets and larger paper continued to be printed via stone (and later aluminum plate) lithography.

In 1926 the radio made its appearance and it had a direct impact on the movie industry. Although a few motion pictures had used sound as early as the late 1890s, it was very difficult to synchronize the sound to the action on the film.

In the mid–1920s, Bell Telephone Laboratories developed a system that could coordinate the sound with the action being projected. In 1926, Warner Brothers experimented with this system, known as Vitaphone, in their movie *Don Juan*. *Don Juan* was actually a silent film with recorded music and sound effects. Warner Bros. released their 1927 *The Jazz Singer* as a silent film with a few songs by star Al Jolson. However, in one scene, Jolson actually spoke a few lines. Shortly thereafter, the Movietone system was introduced. Sound was actually photographed directly on to the film. After moviegoers were exposed to this new sound-on-record method, they demanded only sound pictures.

The popularity of these new "talkies" was so great that movie attendance in the United States increased from 60 million people in 1927 to 110 million two years later. With attendance figures skyrocketing, the public demanded more movies. More movies meant more competition, and more competition meant more advertising dollars and more movie posters.

The appearance of movie posters would soon change dramatically, due to a new color offset printing process developed by Morgan Litho Company. This process made it possible to photograph the artwork provided by studios through screens separated by color. While not as colorful as the stone lithography posters, the color offset process produced sharper images. Over the next twenty years, the two processes would continue to be used. However, by the 1940s, color offset would replace stone lithography for all poster printing.

The 1930s

The 1930s would usher in the time known in the movie industry as the "Golden Age of Movies." This time period saw the emergence of the great Hollywood musicals, the legendary gangster films and the ever popular horror movies. Sound recording equipment improved during this time, which gave creative directors even greater artistic tools. Some of the greatest films in movie history were released during this decade, culminating in 1939 with one of the biggest money-making films in movie history, *Gone with the Wind*.

At this time, the country was caught in the grips of the "art deco" movement (a twentieth century style of decorative art using geometrical designs and bold colors). Motion picture companies kept the pace with the rest of the country, and the movie posters began to take on the art deco look. The use of dense backgrounds was eliminated, and more white space was created. Varying sizes and styles of lettering were used, and the placement of the letters became more creative.

The movie studio during this period generally produced two styles of the one sheet and half sheets, each with different artwork. These were known as

Style "A" and "B" (used by Paramount Studios); Style "C" or "D" (used by MGM); or, in some cases, "X" and "Y" (used by Universal in the 1930s). There were occasions when more than two styles were released, particularly on major productions.

While the film industry was flourishing in the field of make-believe, the United States was facing the all-too-real prospect of an economic depression. With the country suffering such a tremendous economic blow, many felt that the movie industry would surely be one of the casualties. And although the industry did suffer, it was not nearly as hard hit as most had expected. The public still needed to escape—maybe even more so during this time.

The only real negative effect experienced in the industry was that movie-goers now sought out more cheaply priced tickets, so theatre owners were forced to "play the market." With the cheaper admission tickets, the movie studios chose to cut back on operating costs—one of these being the advertising materials. As a result, movie materials were more cheaply produced, and thus lost some of the lavishness of earlier material.

Movie studios and stars were not the only ones to benefit from the movie industry. A number of service related businesses were also flourishing. Theatres and film exhibitors had to deal with each studio individually to get their movie paper or "accessories" as they were sometimes called. In an attempt to centralize this movie paper distribution, independent regional exhibitor exchanges began cropping up all over the country. These independent exhibitor exchanges would get their paper from the studios, and then buy or rent them to theatres and film exhibitors. The theatres liked dealing with these exchanges because they could get the movie paper from all studios at one location, and had the option to either purchase or rent it.

By 1939, National Screen Service (NSS), which had been cutting and distributing trailers since the 1920s, entered into a contract with Paramount Pictures to begin distribution of their movie paper. Over the next few years, the remaining major studios—Columbia, Loew's, Fox, United Artists, RKO, Universal and Warner Bros., as well as other independent film makers—had also contracted with NSS to handle production and distribution of their movie paper.

In addition to the NSS, there were at one time 28 independent regional theatre exchanges around the country. As the NSS gained more control, court battles ensued between the NSS and these independents. Through a compromise, NSS began distributing to the independents as well as directly to theatres.

In order to control the number of materials going through, NSS instituted a date and number coding system for all the movie advertising paper they handled. The numbering code included the year of distribution and the sequential order of the movie's release. At its peak, 90 percent of all advertising materials were handled through the NSS regional offices.

The 1940s

With the Great Depression only a decade behind, the country faced yet another global crisis—World War II. The movie studios and many of their stars did their part in creating a climate of patriotism, and war movies were the genre of the day. In fact, a number of war documentaries were made starring major movie actors who walked away from motion pictures and joined the ranks of the military. Those stars that did not or could not enlist did their part by making movies about the war. For most of this decade, war movies dominated the screens.

The movie industry, which suffered little in comparison to other businesses, was forced to make cost-cutting adjustments—and they chose to make the cuts primarily in their advertising budgets. With a worldwide shortage of paper, many studios used the lesser grade of paper utilized by the newspapers. Some were also printed on the reverse side of old war maps.

By the late 1940s and with World War II now several years behind, the world was introduced to a new entertainment medium—the television. By the end of this decade, television had attracted a large number of moviegoers. The studios responded by reducing the number of films released. Many directors, stars, producers, and others involved in movie making soon found themselves without contracts.

The 1950s

With the return of the GIs from World War II, and a public that wanted more fantasy, the movie studios changed their movie subject matter from the war to science fiction, comedy, and B drive-in movies. Although introduced in 1933, the drive-in theatre reached its peak during the 1950s with over 4,060 screens in the United States.

Television continued to bite into the movie industry's profits. It was no longer necessary to leave your home for viewing pleasure. To combat the "comfort of your own living room" thinking pattern, the movie industry experimented with a number of new wide-screen projection processes. Two such processes, known as CinemaScope and Todd-AO, allowed movies to be shown bigger, more spectacularly and for a more expensive ticket price. These processes were ideal for such epics as *Ben-Hur* and *Cleopatra*. Another lure used by the movie studios was the 3-D movie, along with special 3-D viewing glasses. William Castle, the master of the gimmick production, was bringing audiences back to the theatres by offering them "barf bags" and "buzzer seats."

"Fan magazines" also made their appearance during this time period. *Photoplay* and *Movie Mirror* were two of the pioneers in this area, and their magazines were replete with color photographs of all major movie stars. Movie companies adopted this style of advertising, and soon movie posters began to look more like color photographs, using tinted photographs and large stock lettering. With the number of cars on the roads, posters were designed to be seen from long distances. Stone lithograph movie posters were now a thing of the past.

The 1960s

The most popular movies of the early 1960s were teen oriented. Teen idols from the world of rock & roll successfully crossed over into movie stardom, mostly through the genre known as "beach movies." The Elvis musicals were also extremely popular. Action movies grew in popularity, particularly with the introduction of the infamous Agent 007, James Bond.

Social mores began to change with the mid–1960s. Movie studios were not held to the same strict censorship guidelines as television. As such, more and more adult oriented movies were produced, introducing the movie public to nudity, profanity and excessive violence. Desegregation and the Vietnam War created an atmosphere of social consciousness, and movie makers had to address these issues through their films.

Movie posters during this time mirrored the changing social climate. The posters from the teen oriented movies were normally simple in their artwork design, featuring full length shots of the major stars. Posters from the action movies usually featured the hero, sometimes in a series of dangerous situations. As the 1960s progressed, the posters began to reflect the changing attitudes toward violence and sex. The use of photographs were replacing the painted artwork common in the early years.

The 1970s

The early 1970s were mostly a continuation of the late 1960s. The most significant change came in the area of movies with African American casts. Up to this time, movies with black actors and actresses were distributed only through a chain of theatres patronized by blacks. However, with the changing attitudes toward race, several black action and adventure movies crossed over into the main theatres. Before long, the racial lines disappeared, and black cast movies became common features in major theatres.

The 1970s brought *The Godfather, Rocky, Star Wars, Jaws* and *Star Trek.* This was a springboard into the era of the blockbusters—the 1980s.

The movies posters of the 1970s continued the principal use of photography. Drawing and painting styles were still being used occasionally, and artists like Amsel, Frazetta and Peak lent their names to some of the more popular film posters of this era.

Movie posters from the *Star Wars* and *Star Trek* movies were extremely popular and were responsible for making movie poster collectors out of many fans. Movie posters were now being printed on a clay-coated paper which gave them a glossy finish smooth to the touch.

The 1980s

In the 1980s, moviegoers witnessed great advances in the development and use of special effects. Special effects were the key to the success of the major box office smashes of the 1980s, including *The Empire Strikes Back* (1980), *Raiders of the Lost Ark* (1981), *E.T.* (1982), *Return of the Jedi* (1983), *Ghostbusters* (1984), *Back to the Future* (1985), *Who Framed Roger Rabbit?* (1988) and *Batman* (1989).

By the 1980s, the National Screen Service lost its control over the movie paper industry, leaving only three regional offices remaining in operation. This fact, along with the advent of the multi-screen complexes, changed drastically the lineup of advertising materials available to theatres.

Prior to this time, most theatres had just one screen and one feature movie. A theatre lobby was covered with various sizes of posters for its one movie. With more screens and more movies, the advertising space in the theatre lobby now had to be divided equally among all films being shown. As a consequence, movie studios opted to phase out some of these old standards and introduce a more versatile "mini sheet" which could be produced in any smaller size. This mini sheet could take the place of any of the smaller sizes, since there was no standard size.

The video rental market, which began gaining popularity during the 1980s, gave movie producers another avenue for increasing profits. No longer did movie studios have to rely on theatre box office receipts to make money. Video rental income now figured heavily in weighing the success or failure of a film.

Since video rentals also rely on advertising, a new line of video materials were introduced. Video posters similar to the theatre one sheets were distributed to video rental outlets for display. Many studios issued a number of materials strictly for their video market, making it a viable profit alternative for movie studios.

The rise of the video resulted in the demise of movie reissues (sometimes called rereleases). Instead of rereleasing a film to the theatres, movie studios simply released them on videocassette.

The 1990s

The 1990s brought about the computerization of special effects, creating realistic creatures and adventures that before could only be imagined. This decade has brought three of the biggest money making films of all time, *Jurassic Park*, *Batman Forever*, and *Independence Day*, to theatres.

Advances in animation during this decade have resulted in some of the biggest box office successes in movie history, such as *Beauty and the Beast*, *Aladdin*, *The Lion King*, *Pocahontas* and *The Hunchback of Notre Dame*. It has also led to the billion dollar a year merchandising industry.

Although cable and satellite television have gained popularity, movie theatres and video rental outlets continue to profit. To increase control, studios have moved to more licensing, retail stores, and buying television networks and minor studios. Twentieth Century–Fox created the Fox network so Warner Bros. follows and Disney buys ABC.

As far as movie paper is concerned, the one sheet continues to be used extensively today, although some studios have shortened it one inch to 27" × 40". Many of today's studios have opted to use the "mini" sheet. Since the mini sheet is not a standard size, it can be used to replace many of the old favorites, like inserts, half sheets, window cards. Mini sheets are also used as promotional giveaways, as were the heralds in the 1930s and 1940s. Standups, mobiles and counter displays are also very popular. Video advertising materials are also still widely used. In addition, posters made for cable TV and network television movies have also been introduced.

With entertainment retail chains getting contracts to produce reproduction one sheets, a greater influx of British posters and the advancement of quality reproductions, there is more confusion to the novice poster collectors. This trend is likely to continue, making things more and more difficult for the uninformed collector. With the current competitive market, movie studios must rely heavily on their advertising and promotional programs. The movie poster is still viewed as the centerpiece of the advertising paper, and some of today's posters offer the finest in color, art and graphic detail.

If history is indeed a look into the future, the popularity of the movie poster will continue, even in light of the other advertising avenues available. The movie poster has always been the rock on which the movie industry was built—and all indications are that it will continue to be into the future.

The Basics of
Movie Art Collecting

There are several areas of the movie art collecting industry that should be understood by collectors and would-be collectors. This chapter presents an overview of these major areas. Each of the areas and terms are covered in greater detail in the section which follows. It is suggested that this overview chapter be read before proceeding to the Reference Section.

Collectors Should Be Knowledgeable

As part of a basic background in movie art, collectors should become familiar with the following:

- What constitutes "legitimate theatre art" in the eyes of most movie art collectors.
- The different sizes, shapes and forms of movie art.
- The differences between originally released movie materials and those that are reissued/rereleased.
- The factors that determine the condition and market value of movie art.

Other areas of interest require more space for discussion and are therefore covered in their own chapters. They are:

- The differences in American movie posters and those from foreign countries. (See chapter on Foreign Posters.)
- How and where to begin collecting. (See chapter on Getting Started.)
- The proper way to handle and store posters. (See chapter on Getting Started.)
- When a poster needs professional restoration. (See chapter on Getting Started.)
- How to recognize fakes and *not* get taken. (See chapter on Getting Started.)

Determining Authenticity

The first determination that will be made by a would-be collector is whether or not a particular poster is indeed "legitimate theatre art." Legitimate theatre art is a term commonly used among most collectors to represent those materials that are produced by a motion picture studio as part of their advertising and promotional materials. They are printed and distributed solely for use by the theatre. They are not meant to be distributed or sold to the public. They are printed in limited quantities and are meant to be destroyed or returned at the end of the theatre promotion. All movie art is designed to be used as an advertising tool and then discarded when the film ends its run.

Posters that are *not* considered legitimate theatre art generally fall into one of these categories:

- **Commercial** posters which are printed in large quantities for direct sale to the public. These include reprint or reproduction posters which are commercially produced copies of original movie art printed and distributed to direct sale to the public
- **Video** posters which, while not produced for sale to the general public, are printed as advertising materials for use by video movie rental outlets and are not distributed to theatres. Please note, however, that some video posters are finding a market with certain movie art collectors, but are still not considered "theatre art" since they were never distributed directly to theatres.
- **Cable/TV** posters are also not produced for sale to the general public, but are printed by certain cable/TV stations to promote special run movies. These posters are not considered "theatre art" since they are not distributed to theatres. Please note, however, that some cable/TV posters are finding a market with certain movie art collectors, but are still not considered "theatre art" since they were never distributed directly to theatres.
- **Special promotion** posters, such as those that are released by companies not associated directly with the motion picture industry, but are promoting a movie along with a particular product. Please note, however, that some promotional posters are finding a market with certain movie art collectors, but are still not considered "theatre art" since they were never distributed directly to theatres.

There are a group of specialized movie-related posters that actually fall into a gray area of the movie art collecting industry. These include:

Anniversary Issues: Posters that are released either by the movie studios or licensed printers (such as Kilian Enterprises) to commemorate the anniversary of the release date of a particular movie. These are normally produced in limited numbers for sale to the public.

Limited Editions: Posters that are released either by the movie studios or licensed printers (such as Kilian Enterprises or Suncoast Movie Company) in a special limited edition for public sale (such as an anniversary issue).

Special Releases: Special releases are those limited edition posters that are printed in some unusual manner, such as printed on mylar. [*Note:* There are some special theatre posters that can also be placed in this category. These include one sheets that are printed with special effects, such as holograms. In those cases, the posters are legitimate one sheets, but they require special handling.]

While these posters do not meet the strict criteria of "theatre art," they are gaining favor with some collectors.

The Many Forms of Movie Art

Movie art comes in a variety of sizes, printed on different grades of paper. They also come in different types for specific purposes, depending on the overall advertising campaign outlined for a specific movie. The term "movie poster" is used throughout this book in a generic form, and encompasses any or all of these types. A more detailed breakdown by size follows.

Movie Art Sizes

The following is a list of the more standardized types and sizes of movie art that have been used throughout the years.

POSTERS PRINTED ON PAPER

Since first being introduced by Thomas Edison in 1909, the one sheet movie poster has represented the centerpiece on which a movie's paper advertising program was planned. In addition to the one sheet, there were a number of other posters released by the movie studios. The most common posters are as follows:

One Sheet   The first and most widely used poster, the one sheet measures 27" × 41".

Subway   The subway sheet is also known as the "two sheet" although it is not exactly two times the size of the one sheet.

3 Sheet   This poster is exactly three times the size of a one sheet, measuring 41" × 81".

6 Sheet   Measuring 81" × 81", it is approximately six times the size of a one sheet.

12 Sheet   Measuring 9' × 12', it is approximately twelve times the size of a one sheet.

24 Sheet   Measuring 246" × 108", it is 24 times the size of the one sheet.

Mini Sheet   Introduced only recently by movie studios, the mini sheet comes in a variety of sizes, but is always much smaller than the one sheet.

Stock Sheet   Stock sheets, which were generic in nature, were primarily issued for cartoons or other shorts that were provided to the theatres along with feature films.

POSTERS PRINTED ON CARD STOCK

To complement the use of the paper movie poster, movie studios introduced a line of movie materials printed on card stock. The most common are:

Lobby Card   There are three general sizes of lobby cards: standard (11" × 14"), mini (8" × 14") and jumbo (14" × 17"). Standard and mini sized lobby cards generally come in sets of eight numbered cards which may include a title card, several scene cards, and a dead card.

Insert   Inserts measure 14" × 36" and are printed on paper stock thicker than lobby sets but thinner than window cards.

Half Sheet   Measuring 22" × 28", the half sheet presents artwork and credit information horizontally (longer than it is wide).

Window Card   There are three general categories of window cards: standard (14" × 22"); midget (10" × 18") and jumbo (22" × 28" wide). Window cards are printed on the heaviest stock paper and meant to be placed in retail and office windows and tacked to utility poles, walls, etc.

30" × 40"   Printed on heavy stock and measuring 30" × 40", this poster generally has the same artwork as the one sheet.

40" × 60"   Printed on heavy stock, the 40" × 60" generally has same artwork as the one sheet.

Standups   Large free-standing cutout displays for theatre lobbies.

PRESS MATERIALS

Since the beginning of the industry, movie studios have provided theatres and movie distributors with a wide range of press materials that can be used as part of the overall promotional campaign of a film. Since these materials are designed by the advertising departments of major studios and are individualized for the particular movie, these press materials come in a variety of shapes and forms. However, generally speaking, a standard press package would include the following:

Ad Sheets Ad sheets contain a variety of black and white, camera ready ads that can be used by theatres for their newspaper, periodical and magazine advertising.

Campaign Book A typical campaign book includes the standard press information such as full cast, story line, and star biographies, as well as ad sheets, available advertising materials and related items; suggestions for radio spots; promotional games and ideas; contests, promotions, product tie-ins; and movie merchandising ideas. (Sometimes called the "press book.")

Press Book A typical press book is 8½" × 11", approximately 20 to 30 pages stapled, and will contain the full cast listing, major star biographies, a complete story line, and full credit information. Also called a "campaign book" or a "showman's manual."

Press Kit Press kits come in a variety of forms, but most of them come in a standard sized folder. Kits contain the press book and other ad materials that can be used by the theatre to promote the movie. Items that are sometimes included in press kits are stills, slides, buttons, pins, ad slicks and other promotional materials. Sometimes referred to as "campaign kit."

Scene Stills Black and white stills taken by studio photographers and used in newspapers and magazines for advertising.

PROMOTIONAL MATERIALS

Through the years, movie studios used any number of different approaches to advertising their movies. While many of the materials used were unique to a particular movie title, the following is a list of some of the more generally used promotional aids:

Banners Banners can be any size, but normally measure about 3' to 4' in width and 8' to 12' in length, and are printed vinyl or canvas. They are normally hung either inside or outside of a theatre.

Heralds The herald generally measures 5" × 7" and is folded. From the 1920s through the early 1950s, heralds were given as handouts on the street in front of the theatre or to theatre patrons.

Programs Souvenir programs handed out or sold by theatres. While the above list does not include every type of movie art materials ever used, it does represent the most widely available and generally used sizes of movie art.

Movie Art Forms

In addition to the many sizes, movie posters sometimes come in specific forms, mostly designed for particular purposes. These include:

Advance   Advance posters are specially designed to be issued well in advance of a motion picture's debut. In most cases, the artwork differs from that of the regular issue materials. Advances most often come in one sheet or half sheet sizes.

Award   If a poster receives a prestigious award, such as an Academy Award or Cannes Film Festival Award, a studio will issue a version of the regular issue poster with an indication of the award. Depending on when the award was given, these materials may be original or reissued versions.

Combo   Combo posters feature two or more movies on one poster. In some cases, one movie will be highlighted with another just mentioned as an additional feature. These are often reissues.

Double-sided   Many movie posters are printed using a "reverse" printing on the back side. The front of the poster has the artwork in proper format while the back side as a reverse printing of the same artwork.

Featurette   Featurettes are short subject films that are normally shown before a full-length movie. These include cartoons and short subjects. Studios sometimes release a special poster just for the featurette.

Rename   Sometimes a studio will release a movie under one title, and then later rerelease the movie under another title. In many cases, the poster will contain both movie titles, sometimes using terms like "formerly titled" or "a/k/a."

Review   If a particular movie receives good reviews in the press, movie studios will sometimes issue a special poster which will include quotes from the good reviews. These normally do not take the place of the regular issue, but are offered as an alternative.

Serials   Serials (a series of unending chapters tied to one plot that are shown over an extended period of time) were very popular in the 1930s through 1950s. Movie studios normally issued a poster for each chapter of a titled serial.

Special Distribution   Not all films produced are released to mainstream theatres. There are many movies made each year that are written and produced with a special target audience in mind. Movie posters are usually released with these films. This category would include documentaries, independent studio releases, military training films, regional releases, sex education films and X-rated movies.

Styles   To cater to two or more specific audience groups, studios would sometimes issue two different versions of a poster, most often the one sheet or half sheet. These styles are indicated in some way, such as "Style A" or "Style B."

Secondary Printers/Distributors

In the beginning, movie studios produced and printed their own materials. They utilized the services of a number of lithographers around the country. Throughout the years, a number of secondary printers came on the market using a cheaper line of movie materials, particularly for materials that were used in greater numbers. One of the largest of these secondary printers was the Benton Card Company. Many of the Benton materials are found in today's movie art market. Their desirabilty and collectibility are constantly in dispute among hard line and liberal movie poster collectors.

From the 1940s through the 1980s, most major studios turned over the distribution of their movie paper to the National Screen Service (NSS). In order to control the distribution, NSS established a dating and numbering system. This NSS number is normally found in the border of the poster. Materials that were released by secondary printers did not go through NSS for distribution. To many hard line collectors, materials from this period that do not have the "NSS" number are not considered "collectible movie art."

Encore Performances

Over the years, many of the classics have been rereleased to theatres. In many cases, new posters are simultaneously released. While these reissues meet the criteria of legitimate theatre art, there is a difference in the value of the original movie poster and the rereleased version. Determining the difference can be difficult when dealing with posters from the early years. However, there are a number of ways that can be used.

Determining Value

While there is no set way for determining an exact value or condition of a poster, there are some general factors that, when viewed as whole, can give a very good estimate of a poster's condition and potential market value. Of course, the value of the poster is dictated by the theory of supply and demand—and if someone wants a particular poster, they may be willing to pay more than its market value. However, this is not the case in most instances.

Two principal areas should be considered when attempting to place a value on a poster.

The first step is to consider its status in the collector's market. Factors to be considered include:

- A poster's rarity.
- The market demand for that title.
- Recent selling price for that specific title.

The second consideration to be factored in when determining value is the condition of the poster. The condition of a poster is determined by the existence of blemishes or defects somewhere on the poster and the location of those blemishes or defects. Defects or blemishes include: bleedthroughs/seethroughs, creases, fading, folds or fold lines, holes, marks, stains, tears, trimming, and wrinkles.

The area around the poster that is not a part of the poster's artwork is normally considered the *border*. Most defects or blemishes appearing in the border have little or no impact on the poster's value. However, when these defects or blemishes are found in the poster's artwork, then the value is decreased in promotion to the type and size of the defect or blemish.

Determining the condition of a poster is completely "subjective," and is based solely on the individual doing the appraising. However, there are some general guidelines that most collectors employ for trying to grade the condition of the poster. The most common includes a six-grade system:

- Mint
- Near Mint
- Very Good
- Good
- Fair
- Poor

There are two other grading systems that are also used. One divides the condition among nine grades. The other is a letter system normally used by auctions to assess a value.

Obviously, the better condition the poster is in, the higher price it will command. Once all of the factors have been evaluated, a fair estimate can be made of the poster's overall value.

There are a number of other things that can affect the potential value of a poster. If a poster's artwork was done by a well-known artist, such as Norman Rockwell, the poster may be considered more valuable in the eyes of many collectors. Linen-backing, a process of double mounting a poster to linen or cotton backing, can increase the value a poster, as linen-backing usually makes a poster more durable.

The Illustrated Reference section which follows will address each of the items listed above individually. The section is presented in alphabetical order for easy location.

The two other main areas of interest to a collector that is not covered in the Illustrated Reference section are foreign posters and how to get started. These are addressed individually under their own chapter headings.

Illustrated Reference
to Major Terms,
Concepts and Companies

Ad Sheets/Slicks

An ad sheet, or slick as it is called in the printing industry, is a page or pages of camera ready ads laid out by the movie studios and sent to theatres for their use in placing ads in newspapers and magazines for a particular film.

Ad sheets/slicks are normally pages either bound or loosely placed within the press book or press kit. For larger promotions, the ad sheets may be 20 to 30 pages bound separately and called "ad pads" or "ad supplements." These sheets contain a series of black and white camera ready ads in various sizes and types. Like clip art, the ads can be cut out of the ad sheet/slicks and sent in to the newspaper or magazine. Some ads will contain an area where the theatre can put their name and show times.

Underneath each ad is the display size information used by newspapers and magazines (that is, 4 cols × 150 line—43 inches). Ad sheets/slicks sometimes contain pages of different clip out slogans or "slugs" such as "Now Showing" or "Starts Friday." These slogans can be pasted on the bottom of the ad.

In short, the ad sheets/slicks provide all the ad materials and information that is needed by a theatre to run an effective newspaper or magazine ad campaign.

See also: Press Books; Press Kits; Movie Art/Paper

Advances

When a movie studio wants to create an early interest in a particular movie, they will issue a series of advertising materials to theatres and film distributors well in *advance* of the film's actual release date. These materials are

AD 202 B 2 COL. x 75 LINES = 150 LINES

AD 102BB - 1 col. x
14 lines = 14 lines

AD 101BB - 1 col. x
28 lines = 28 lines

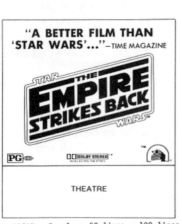

AD 203BB - 2 col. x 50 lines = 100 lines

AD 204BB - 2 col. x 25 lines = 50 lines

Samples of various ad slicks with column information.

generally referred to as "advances." They are also sometimes called "teasers." The sole purpose of these materials is to alert moviegoers that the movie is about to be released and to generate pre-release publicity in the community.

The use and style of the advance sheets vary greatly from studio to studio; and within each studio, from film to film. The decision as to whether to use advance materials, and what form those materials will take, is determined by the promotional plan that is outlined by the movie studios' advertising and promotion departments. Each film is unique, and the studios plan their marketing approach differently with each title.

The movie studios send press kits to the theatres well in advance of the release of a film. Once a film is booked by that theatre, advance sheets are then sent to the theatre for use. Most advance materials are released in the form of one sheets, two sheets, banners and standups.

For advance promotion, a studio may choose to use the same artwork on their advance and regular release materials. In some cases, the same poster art will be used, but the advance sheet will carry a tag line indicating that it is "coming soon" or "soon to be released" or even give a specific date. In still other cases, the artwork of an advance sheet will be identical to that of the regular issue, but will not include the credit information. In situations that involve films with larger promotional budgets, completely different advance sheets will be designed to complement the regular ad materials. When dealing with films that are destined to be "mega-hits," some studios will issue a series of advances.

For example, for the movie *Bram Stoker's Dracula*, the studio issued a series of advances. When the regular one sheet was issued, it had totally different artwork. On the other hand, with the mega-hit *Jurassic Park*, Universal Studio issued an advance poster which had the simple "Jurassic" emblem (with no credit information) and slogan on the bottom. The studio used this same simple artwork, *with* the credit information, as the regular issue.

Distinguishing Advance and Regular Advertising Materials: While all of these movie advertising materials are unique, more often than not advance sheets can be spotted by simply checking for one or more of the following hints:

- Words such as "Advance," "Teaser" or "Adv" located on the bottom border of the poster.
- Slogans such as "Coming Soon" or "Coming This Summer" which are sometimes printed across the top, but more often across the bottom.
- Projected release dates which are sometimes printed across the top, but more often across the bottom.
- Limited, subdued or simple graphics and/or containing very limited or no credit information.
- Nebulous terms such as "Beware" or "It's Here" with no movie title or credit information.

Collectibility: Collectors who base their collections on title, genre or subject

Batman **advance. Notice the date and the emblem.**

are more drawn to advance materials because advance materials complement their poster collections. Some collectors prefer to collect advance materials because these materials are in the theatres a shorter period of time and because the studios normally produce fewer numbers of them. Many collectors prefer

Batman regular issue. Note the addition of names of stars, title, credits, and studio logo.

Advance sheet for *An Eye for an Eye.*

the artwork and the limited credit information that are found on some advance materials. This is particularly true with some of the later Walt Disney animated feature films.

See also: Banners; One Sheet; Standups

Anniversary Issues

The public's constant desire for more collectible movie materials on certain classic films has resulted in a class of collectible movie posters known as "Anniversary Issues." These posters, which are traditionally very beautiful and elaborate, mark the anniversary of the original release date of certain all-time favorite movies, such as *Casablanca, Snow White, Fantasia,* and *Star Wars.*

These anniversary issues are designed not only to pay homage to the great film classics, but also to keep their popularity alive and growing with newer and younger movie audiences. Because of this, the producers of these posters (which can either be the studios themselves or licensed printers) normally go to great lengths to ensure that these issues are exquisitely designed and printed. In many cases, in addition to their overall aesthetic beauty, some anniversary issues may:

- Be printed in limited numbers to make them instantly collectible.
- Have each poster individually numbered.
- Be designed and drawn by well known and nationally recognized commercial artists.
- Be printed on gold or silver mylar.

This 25th anniversary release of United Artists is a reissue of the awards style.

While not all anniversary issues will contain one or more of these special effects, most of them will possess extraordinary and beautiful artwork.

On some occasions, the studio will turn to artwork that was created during the original campaign but never released on any prior poster production and use it for the anniversary issue.

Who Produces Them?: Many of the anniversary issues are released by the movie studios who initially produced the films (or who currently owns the rights). These include such popular issues as *Fantasia 50th Anniversary* (released by Walt Disney Studios); *Star Wars First Anniversary* (released by George Lucas Studios); and the *25th Anniversary Midnight Cowboy* (released by United Artists).

In some cases, anniversary issues are designed and released by private printing companies who obtain the approval and rights to the issue from the movie studio who holds the rights to the film. One of the more popular of these printers is Kilian Enterprises of Wichita, Kansas. Jeff Kilian has been responsible for the design and release of a number of collectors' favorites, including the extremely popular *Star Wars* trilogy anniversary series posters, consisting of the 5th, 10th and 15th anniversaries.

Anniversary Issues Are Not Usually Rereleases/Reissues: These anniversary issues are special edition releases and should not be confused with reissues/rereleases. Anniversary issues are usually released for sale to the public; reissues/rereleases, on the other hand, are "legitimate theatre art" and are intended solely for distribution to theatres. Reissues/rereleases always accompany the rerelease of the movie itself to the theatres or film distributors. Anniversary issues are *not normally associated* with the rerelease of the film to theatres. The anniversary issues are most commonly released to commemorate the anniversary of the movie's original release date. If an anniversary issue is released at the same time the movie is rereleased to theatres, it is merely a coincidence.

Exception: An exception to this involves Walt Disney's planned rerelease of its classic *Fantasia*. The movie one sheet that was released with the film carried a tag line proclaiming *Fantasia*'s 50th Anniversary. However, because this poster was released specifically as the advertising one sheet to go to theatres to promote the rerelease of *Fantasia*, it clearly meets the criteria for "legitimate theatre art" and is therefore a rerelease poster.

Collectibility: Anniversary issues are normally *not* original "theatre art" (that is, materials released when a movie debuts at the theatres). As such, to most hard line movie art collectors, these are not legitimate movie art. They are, however, sought after by some more liberal minded movie poster collectors for the following reasons:

(1) Anniversary issues are only released for perennial, all-time favorites; therefore, there is always a steady market for these materials among older and newer audiences.

(2) Anniversary issues are quite often more elaborate and beautiful than the original "theatre materials" and therefore are more desirable because of their aesthetic beauty. Some anniversary issues are printed on mylar (a strong polyester film) which makes them not only more beautiful but much more durable (for example, the *Star Wars Tenth Anniversary* is printed on silver mylar).

(3) Anniversary issues are printed in limited quantities, making them harder to attain.

(4) Anniversary issues are usually individually numbered. These numbers are most commonly located on the bottom right hand corner. If the anniversary is issued by a licensee, it is usually numbered, if by the studio it is not.

Because most of these anniversary issues are printed for a limited time and in limited quantities, and are quite often individually numbered, they would most aptly fit into the category of "Limited Editions." If, as in the case of the *Exception* listed above, the poster is released to the theatres as an advertising one sheet to promote the rerelease of a movie, then the poster falls in the category of reissues/rereleases.

See also: Kilian Enterprises; Limited Editions; Rereleases/Reissues; Special Issues

Artists

Although most major studios have their own art departments, they sometimes contract with well-known and recognizable commercial artists to produce the artwork used in their movie advertising materials. Names such as Alvin, Rockwell, Vargas, Crandall, Klee, Petty, Hirschfeld, Amsel, Drew, Peak, the Hildebrandt brothers, Soulie, Frazetta, Craig, Lettick and Boris grace the artwork of many posters. The artists sign the artwork, and their signature is then reproduced on the artwork.

It is most unfortunate that during the early days of America's motion picture industry, movie studios would not allow artwork to be signed by the artists. In many cases where an artist was known for a particular style, the movie studios required that the artist design the work in a style "unlike his own." In this way, the artist could not be identified by his "well-known" style. It is believed that many of the finest commercial artists of that time period contributed to some of the earliest of movie posters, and yet these works were unsigned and, in most cases, the artist remains unknown.

While the American studios chose to keep silent on this issue, their European counterparts took an entirely different approach. From the beginning, European movie studios contracted with commercial artists, allowing them to sign and acknowledge their contributions. Fortunately, it did not take long for American

Classic Norman Rockwell style artwork for *Cinderfella*.

movie companies to join their European counterparts by commissioning famous commercial artists and allowing them to sign and style their work.

Collectibility: Many movie art collectors are interested only in posters whose artwork is signed by a recognizable commercial artist. As such, even though the movie itself may not have been popular or a commercial success, the movie posters are sought after because of their signed artwork. In today's movie art market, many collections are based solely on a particular artist. In many instances, it is the least expensive way to own an art piece designed by such a talent as Vargas or Rockwell. Because certain artists are well-known to movie poster collectors, their posters will command higher prices than those of lesser-known commercial artists.

Quite often a studio will issue two different styles of posters, one with painted artwork and one utilizing photographs. In these cases, the artist version will command slightly higher dollars than the poster utilizing photography.

Awards

Awards posters are those that contain an indication somewhere on the body of the poster that the movie has either been nominated for or given a prestigious industry award. In most cases, the awards posters are one sheet size. However, movie studios have released "awards" materials in other standard sizes.

When an American movie is either nominated for or given an American movie industry award, such as an Academy Award or Golden Globe Award, and it is not in theatres at the time of the award, many movie studios will rerelease the movie to the theatres. When this happens, the studios generally issue a new set of advertising materials, and these new materials will contain some reference to the particular award won. In cases where the movie is still in theatres, studios will pull all original materials off the market and release new ones with the awards notation. In either case, the new movie posters will contain notations such as "Academy Award Winner," "Nominated for 8 Academy Awards," or "Golden Globe's Best Picture Award." Since these awards are usually given to films *after they are released to the American theatres*, any materials with awards references that are rereleased to the theatres are considered to collectors to be "reissues/rereleases" and not original movie paper. The poster's original artwork usually has to be changed or reduced in order to accommodate the award proclamation.

There are cases, however, in which a poster may contain a notation of an award and be an *original* issue. This occurs, for example, when an American movie is first introduced to a foreign film festival, such as the Cannes Film Festival in France. If the movie has not already been released to the American market and has won such an award, the original advertising materials may contain a slogan or symbol indicating that it has won a foreign award. These materials are considered to be *original* and command top dollar as such.

Distinguishing Original from Reissue Awards Poster: To decide if an awards poster is an original or reissue/release, consider the following:

- Was the award given *after the movie's release to the theatres*?
- Was the movie exhibited at a foreign film festival *before it was released to theatres*?

In short, if the movie received the award before it was released to the market and before advertising materials were issued, then the movie poster containing the awards notation is considered to be an original. If the award is given after the movie's release to the theatres, even though it may still have been showing in theatres, the new movie materials are considered reissues/rereleases.

Exception: If a film receives a smaller industry award (not as prestigious as other awards), the studios may choose not to reissue new materials, but instead issue a sticker that can be placed on the regular movie materials.

Collectibility: Award posters are considered collectible movie art, particularly those from classic films. If the poster is not an original issue and movie materials were pulled from the market in order to reissue new award noted materials, then the original "unmarked" posters should have greater value to collectors since fewer remained on the market. If the awards poster is the original issue, then its value will be determined by market demand. To get a higher price, some dealers will try to up the price saying it's the original year.

See also: Rereleases/Reissues

Banners

SUMMARY OF FACTS

Size: Varies; normally 3' to 4' wide and 8' to 12' long on vinyl, canvas.

History: First used in the 1930s.

Purpose: They were used in theatre lobbies, on balconies, and other ad spaces inside and outside theatres, such as bus, train and subway depots.

Current Usage: Widely used in American and foreign theatre markets.

Notes: Extremely durable in all weather conditions because they are printed on vinyl or canvas.

Banners were introduced into the market in the 1930s. They were primarily offered for major motion pictures, and were very popular with movie exhibitors because of their versatile nature. Because they were printed on vinyl or canvas materials, they were easily adaptable to both indoor and outdoor displays.

Banners vary in size, normally measuring about 3' to 4' in width to 8' to 12' in length, and are printed vinyl or canvas. Because they are more weather-resistant than paper or card stock, they can be used liberally both indoors and outdoors. It is quite common for banners to have two reinforced holes across the top and bottom for hanging purposes. The majority of the banners are printed horizontally, but occasionally some are designed to be hung vertically. The banner's artwork can be very detailed; however, the artwork on most banners is very simple.

Current Usage: Banners are still a popular form of advertising by the major motion picture studios today in American and foreign theatre markets. Banners can be released as advance or regular issues.

Collectibility: Banners are legitimate movie art and are considered movie collectibles. Only a small quantity of banners are issued. So, banners are a lot harder to obtain, making them more desirable to some collectors. Banners from Disney Studio animation releases are extremely popular with collectors.

See also: Advances; Movie Art/Paper

Benton Card Company

Unlike most forms of movie art, window cards were not meant for viewing within the theatre, but were instead intended for mass distribution—to be displayed in business windows and on telephone poles throughout a neighborhood or community. As such, theatres and film exhibitors normally purchased these in bulk since they required more than one or two copies.

In the late 1940s, the Benton Card Company arranged with American International Pictures to design and print window cards for their movie releases. The Benton Card Company produced a line of window cards which were designed and distributed as a less expensive alternative to the advertising materials which were being distributed by the movie companies through the National Screen Service (NSS). The National Screen Service, as well as a small number of other national print companies, published full color window cards. Benton cards were produced in limited colors on a cheaper card stock, making them a less expensive alternative for smaller theatres, particularly those in rural areas.

In addition to window cards, Benton Card Company also offered a line of inexpensive heralds to theatres.

Differences in Benton and NSS Window Cards: One major difference between the window cards produced by Benton and those produced by the National Screen Service is the number of colors used. Most Benton window cards were printed using one color (monotone), two colors (duotone) or in some cases three colors (tritone). The National Screen Service, as well as the other major movie material printers, utilized full color presses, making their materials much more vivid.

Another major difference between the Benton cards and those of NSS is in the quality of the card stock used. Benton kept their printing costs down by using a cheaper, thicker card stock. The NSS utilized a higher grade of thinner card stock.

The simplest way to determine if a window card is a Benton original is to check for the tag "Benton Card Company," which was printed along the bottom of all of their window cards.

Benton Product Line: The Benton Card Company is still active in printing window cards for music and other entertainment events. As far as movie-related materials are concerned, they offer the following types of material:

ORIGINALS

Benton Card Company originals were printed on thick heavy card stock, and the backside is shaded gray. An original will carry the tag "BENTON CARD COMPANY, INC., BENSON, N.C." usually centered across the bottom of the window card.

BENTON CARD COMPANY, INC., BENSON, N. C.

OLDER REPRINTS

Over the years Benton Card Company would reissue some of their window cards. These reissues were printed on the same old heavy card stock as were the originals, utilizing the same printing plates. The "older" reprints are distinguished from their original counterparts by a handwritten notation somewhere on the bottom of the card. This notation contains a year, a slash (/) and a stock number (for example, 1949/844). The "Benton Card Company" tag is found on some reprints, but not all. These reprints look so much like the originals that some of these reprints were mistakenly sold as originals.

NEW REPRINTS

In the 1980s, when paper companies quit manufacturing the older, thicker card stock, Benton began reprinting their window cards on a newer, thinner, glossier card stock. These newer, more colorful reprints carry the letter "R" on the lower border along with the stock number.

STARRING
PAUL CHRISTIAN · PAULA RAYMOND · CECIL KELLAWAY
KENNETH TOBEY · JACK PENNICK
Screen Play by LOU MORHEIM and FRED FREIBERGER

Photography by Jack Russell, A.S.C. · Associate Producer BERNARD W. BURTON
Technical Effects Created by RAY HARRYHAUSEN · Music by David Buttolph

715-R   BENTON CARD CO., BENSON, NC

Suggested by the
SATURDAY
EVENING POST
story by
RAY BRADBURY

↖   ↗

Collectibility: Because the Benton Card Company was considered a "secondary" printing company, many long-time collectors shy away from collecting Benton window cards. Benton window cards do not command the same dollar value as their NSS counterparts, even though they are the same age, and may be identical to the NSS versions.

For example, the window card released by NSS for the film *Hi-De-Ho* (1947) was printed in three color. The Benton version was identical—same age, artwork, three color, and pictures. The only differences are that the Benton version was printed on a thicker, cheaper card stock and contained a different tag line; however, for all intents and purposes, they are identical until they reach the collector's market. The Benton Card Company version of the *Hi-De-Ho* window card is valued by most collectors at approximately 10 percent to 20 percent of the retail value of the NSS window card. Benton cards are finding a market, however, with newer collectors who want to collect older materials at a less expensive price.

See also: Heralds; National Screen Service; Secondary Printers; Window Card

Bleedthroughs/See-Throughs

A bleedthrough occurs when writing (particularly markers), other marks or stains that are on the back of the poster are absorbed into the paper and are then seen on the front. A see-through occurs when tape, marks or stains, particularly writing on the back side of the poster, particularly with a black grease pencil, can be "seen" on the front of the poster. The pencil does not "bleed" through the poster, but it creates a dark shadow which can be seen from the front when held up to the light.

A see-through can only be seen if the poster is held up to the light, but a bleedthrough can be seen on the front in any light or position.

Causes: Bleedthroughs/see-throughs can occur for any number of reasons, but some of the most common ones are:

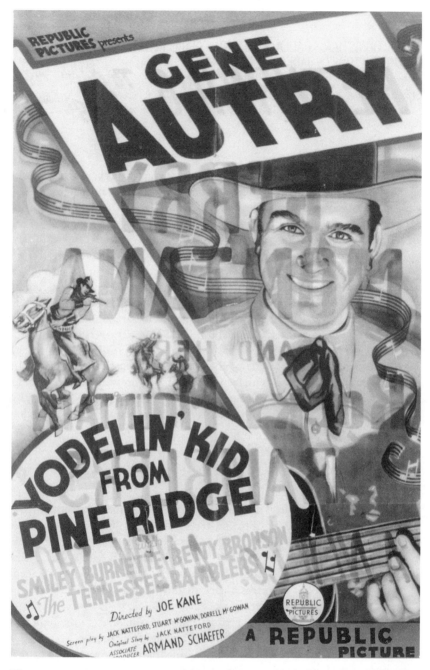

Theatre manager used the back of the poster as a billboard, ruining a fine poster. (From the collection of John Hazelton.)

- It was not uncommon for theatre managers to place posters in the windows of the theatres and to use the back side of the poster (the side which was seen from the inside of the theatre) to write information such as coming attractions and show times, or to tape other pictures or notes on the back of the poster. In general, the poster itself was used as a bulletin board. In order for the writing to be visible from a distance, heavy markers were used, which sometimes bled into the paper, or, even if the ink didn't bleed through, the writing can be seen on the front.
- Some bleedthroughs and see-throughs are the result of using different types of tape to repair holes or tears in the poster. Some adhesive tapes are very acidic, and the acid will eventually eat through the poster. Less acidic tapes may not actually bleed through the paper, but can create see-throughs.

Effect on Poster's Value: The location, size and prominence of the bleedthrough/see-through as seen on the front will determine just how much value the poster loses because of its existence. If the bleedthrough/see-through occurs on the border only, the value of the poster is not adversely affected. However, if the bleedthrough/see-through affects the artwork, the value of the poster is greatly diminished.

Repair/Restoration Options: If bleedthroughs are the result of an alcohol-based marker (such as a Magic Marker), the mark is absorbed into the color fiber of the poster. The only way to correct this type of bleedthrough is to remove the mark through a controlled bleaching process, and then to recolor the pigment of the area of the poster where the original color was bleached out. *This must be done by a professional restorer.*

Tape can sometimes be removed through a continuous controlled washing and flushing process. *This too must be done by a professional restorer.*

See-throughs can only be seen when there is light behind the poster. To eliminate the "shadow" effect of a see-through, simply frame the poster, eliminating the light source.

See also: Condition

Borders

The area located around, but not a part of, the artwork of a poster is generally considered its border. Just as the artwork of the posters differs, so do the borders. Most often white but sometimes black strips are present around the outer edge of the poster. Sometimes, there are only top or bottom borders, or borders just on the sides. And, in some cases, a poster will have no obvious border whatsoever. All movie paper sizes *include* the area considered the border.

For example, a one sheet is normally sized 27" × 41", which includes the border area. If the border is trimmed from the poster, it is no longer 27" × 41".

Since the mid–1980s, a growing number of studios are opting to bleed the picture artwork all the way to the edge of the paper on the one sheet, thus eliminating the border. To do this, printers have to shorten the poster, so a number of the newer one sheets are measuring 27" × 40". Before this time, all one sheets were 27" × 41". A one sheet in any other size would be looked upon as a possible fake.

The shortening of the one sheet creates a problem with collectors. Defects and blemishes on borders were acceptable to collectors. However, by eliminating an obvious border, any defects or blemishes on the poster now affect the poster's artwork, thus affecting their value.

Border Defects/Blemishes: Since the border of a poster is considered the area surrounding the artwork and is not a part of the artwork, common blemishes, tears and marks on the border generally do not adversely affect the overall value of the poster. However, when the blemishes, tears or marks start in the border but continue into the poster's artwork, the value and collectibility of the poster could be significantly affected. In this case, further consideration as to condition will have to be made.

Trimming also has a negative effect on the poster's value. Border damage should be repaired or framed out.

See also: Condition; One Sheet; Printing Processes/Lithographers; Trimming; chapter on Getting Started

Cable/Network TV Posters

Promotional Materials for TV Movies: A growing number of the movies that are produced are *not* distributed to the theatres, but instead are shown as "first-run" movies on cable movie stations such as HBO and Showtime, or as "mini-series" on networks such as ABC and FOX. There are other cases where movies may have had their first run through the theatres, but then the exclusive TV broadcast rights are purchased by a cable or network TV channel. In some of these instances, movie posters and other promotional items are sometimes released by the studios and sent to the cable distributors and or network affiliates for use in promoting the movie.

The posters that are released in association with TV-related movies are in many cases very similar to theatre one sheets. They may be an inch or two smaller in size, but are usually distinguishable by the station's logo, such as "HBO" or "Showtime," or network TV's "ABC-TV" or "FOX-TV" somewhere on the poster.

Collectibility: Even though these posters are not "legitimate" theatre sheets, they have found favor with certain collectors for a number of reasons.

The TV poster from "Lois & Clark" is cropping up on dealer lists around the country.

Some collectors base their collections on subjects, genres or stars. If a certain star happens to make a cable/TV movie, and this is the only poster that exists for the movie, then to someone who collects art on that star the poster is desirable. Other collectors consider these cable/TV posters collectible if they are the "only" poster printed for that particular movie and there are no "theatre" counterparts. Because these posters are only printed for the cable/TV offices, they are printed in extremely limited numbers, making them desirable to some collectors because there are so few around. However, in cases where the movie made a theatre run and then is later shown on a TV channel, the "TV" poster is generally not considered as "collectible" to any collector, unless of course they are collecting the poster for the movie's stars or want to collect *all* posters ever released on a certain title.

To hard line collectors, these posters *are not* "legitimate theatre art" and are therefore not considered collectible as movie art.

Another rapidly growing interest is the collection of series posters. They are usually only produced at the season premieres to promote the series. Some of these posters have become extremely popular, depending upon the popularity of the series itself. Such series include "The X-Files," "Lois & Clark," and "Duckman."

See also: Video Posters

Campaign Book/Special Edition

SUMMARY OF FACTS

Size: Varied.

Binding: Hardbound.

History: Introduced in the 1920s.

Purpose: To provide a complete movie campaign or plan for the exhibitors.

Current Usage: Discontinued in 1940s.

Notes: Extremely rare. Not to be confused with traditional press book.

During the 1920s through the 1940s, some of the major studios issued a full color campaign book for major motion pictures. These were distributed in lieu of the standard press books (which are also sometimes called campaign books).

This deluxe version of the campaign book came in a variety of sizes and styles. They were normally printed in full color and were hardbound. The campaign book included the standard press information, such as cast, crew, story line and facts about the production. They also contained campaign suggestions, such as specific ideas for promotions, contests, newspaper and radio advertising and promotional materials available.

Note: The term "campaign book" is also used to describe the variety of press materials that are issued by the studios to theatres. This term is commonly used interchangeably throughout the movie art industry with other terms such as "press book," "showman's manual," "campaign manual," etc. Because each studio designed and released unique press materials for each movie, they also used different terms to describe them. These are described in more detail in the Campaign Kit, Press Book and Press Kit entries.

Current Usage: The studios discontinued the use of a hardbound campaign book in the 1940s.

Collectibility: These hardbound campaign books are extremely rare and are very valuable if in good condition.

See also: Campaign Kits; Press Kit; Press Books

Campaign Kits

SUMMARY OF FACTS

Size: Varies, notebook style.

History: Introduced in the 1910s.

Purpose: To provide a complete movie campaign or plan for the exhibitors.

Current Usage: Used today in the form of press kits.

Notes: Although they are sometimes referred to as "press kits," legitimate "campaign kits" contained more promotional aids, such as buttons and posters, in addition to the normal press information found in a press kit.

Campaign kits were distributed by studios as early as the 1910s. Their main purpose was to assist movie theatres and exhibitors with ideas for a successful movie campaign. Since the success of the movie had a direct financial impact on the studios, it was very important to them that movie theatres and exhibitors had all the tools at their fingertips to promote a successful exhibition.

Although they are sometimes mistakenly used interchangeably with "press book," the campaign book is more comprehensive and elaborate than the press book. A typical campaign book includes the standard press information such as full cast, story line, and star biographies, as well as ad sheets, a breakdown of other advertising materials that are available; radio commercial ideas; promotional games and ideas; contests, promotions, product tie-ins; and movie merchandising ideas. Many campaign kits include materials such as buttons, giveaways, posters and negatives. In short, a campaign book contains everything that a theatre would need to conduct a successful movie campaign.

Early campaign kits contained an extensive amount of materials for the theatre owners to use to plan their movie campaign—even hardbound campaign books and a wide variety of materials were sometimes provided, primarily for major productions. As the years went on and advertising budgets decreased, the campaign kits and books grew smaller. They were initially used to give the illusion of grandeur, but slowly evolved into showman's manuals and the present-day press kit.

Current Usage: The campaign kit of yesteryear is no longer issued by studios. However, a more compact version of the campaign kit, which is known as the press kit, is widely used by all motion picture companies. The term "campaign kit" is rarely used in today's movie market. All press materials are now referred to as "press kits."

Collectibility: Because the campaign book contained so much information about a movie and its cast, campaign books are very popular with some collectors. In many cases, these books are the only evidence of exactly what posters and related materials were released for a particular film. In addition, the campaign book can provide a means for determining the age of a poster if none is shown on the face of the poster. They are extremely important to dating of movie materials.

See also: Ad Sheets/Slicks; Campaign Book/Special Edition; Movie Art/ Paper; Press Books; Press Kits; Scene Stills

Combo Posters

Sometimes a studio will offer a package deal of multiple movie titles together for one showing. For this special showing, they produce a poster showing the combination of movies. These posters are referred to as combos. The majority of the combo posters were issued for "B" grade movies, particularly those shown at drive-ins.

The two most common sizes of combo posters are one sheets and window cards, although they have been produced in other sizes. The manner in which the movies are displayed on the posters vary, based on how the movie studio wants to promote each film. For example, the top half may have the artwork of one movie, while the bottom half has the artwork of the other. Other posters are split vertically down the middle, each movie's artwork being presented equally. In still other cases, the studio may focus more on one movie, with just a notation on the bottom saying "also featuring."

Note: A combo poster always reflects two full length feature presentations. This should not be confused with posters that have a tag indicating a "featurette." A featurette is a short film clip that is shown before a feature movie. A poster with a tag like this is not considered a combo.

Combo posters are sometimes released for studio-promoted double features (as opposed to double feature presentations planned by an individual theatre). Although rare today, double features were extremely common prior to the 1980s and combo posters were used more frequently during that time.

Collectibility: Combo posters are normally reissues and rarely command the same dollars as their individually issued counterparts. The exceptions would be where different or unusual artwork is found on the combo poster that is not on the individually issued poster. In these cases, the poster would be considerably more valuable, depending on the movie titles.

See also: Featurette; Rereleases/Reissues

A combo reissue poster of two full-length horror movies, *Blood Lust* and *Blood Mania*.

Commercial

The category of commercial posters represents the thousands of posters that are designed, issued and distributed for direct sale to the public. They come in all types and sizes about literally thousands of subjects. They can feature movie stars, sports stars, animated characters, cars, models, etc.

One small area of commercial posters is dedicated to the movie industry. Because of public demand for movie related materials, some commercial printing companies issue a series of posters known as "commercial movie art."

Dangerous Years is Marilyn Monroe's first movie! A National Screen Service jumbo window card (22" × 28").

What Is Commercial Movie Art? The main factor that differentiates legitimate movie art from commercially produced posters is that legitimate movie art is never intended for public sale. They represent advertising materials that are designed for and distributed to the theatres to advertise a particular film. Legitimate theatre art is printed in limited numbers, only the number needed to accommodate theatres and film exhibitors. Commercial posters, on the other hand, are printed en masse, and can be reproduced whenever there is a demand.

Commercial movie art posters are designed to look like legitimate theatre posters. Some may contain the same artwork and credit information. However, contrary to the strict definition of "legitimate theatre art," these posters are distributed directly to outlets for public sale and are never sent to the theatres. These are not advertising materials—they are commercially produced copies of the theatre posters.

Distinguishing Commercial from Legitimate Movie Art. Although they can look identical at first glance, there are a number of ways to determine if a poster is commercially produced.

The most obvious difference is the size of the poster; commercial posters are normally the standard size of 24" × 36" or smaller. Legitimate movie posters are 27" × 41" (or 27" × 40" in some cases). Another major difference can be found in the border of the poster. Commercial posters normally contain a reorder number and the name of the printer. Original movie posters never have a reorder number and rarely contain the name of the printer.

Exception: Theatre posters from some foreign countries sometimes contain the printer's name in the bottom border. See the chapter on Foreign Posters.

Most commercial posters are distributed through chain stores, discount stores and other retail outlets. Legitimate theatre art is normally found in collectible and antique shops; through legitimate movie poster collectors or dealers; or at movie poster auctions and trade shows.

Commercial Movie Art Posters: There are a number of commercial printers who dedicate a good portion of their inventory to movie-related materials. The following are generally considered the country's largest:

• Portal Publishing is arguably the largest distributor of commercial movie art. Portal's commercial movie posters contain the same artwork and credit information as the legitimate theatre counterparts. However, Portal's posters are 24" × 36" or smaller and have the name "Portal Publishing Co." printed on the bottom. They also contain Portal's reorder number.

Even though Portal advertises their posters as "commercial," they are poster distributors and cannot control or monitor what individual stores are saying about their posters. Some Portal posters have shown up in collector shops and erroneously advertised as "legitimate movie art." A quick review of the size and bottom of the poster will classify it as a commercial print. The most confusing Portal is the half sheet (22" × 28") which is the same size as the theatre piece, but it has "Portal Publishing Co." in the bottom border.

• O.S.P. (One Stop Posters) is one of the largest commercial printers in the country. Although Portal focuses more on movie related posters, O.S.P. offers a wider subject range of posters, such as music industry, sports, scenery and comedy. It does have a line of commercial movie art and is the exclusive distributor of Disney animation commercial posters.

• Western Graphics, American Art and Funky are all commercial poster printers who offer some commercial movie art materials, although they do not have the variety of commercial movie art that Portal and O.S.P. offer.

There are, of course, other commercial prints who dabble in commercial movie art. However, the five listed are generally recognized as the leaders in the area of commercial movie art.

This commercial reproduction of a half sheet of *Casablanca* has "Portal Publishing Co." The reorder number appears in lower border of the original.

Quasi-Commercial

There is another category of movie-related posters that does not qualify as legitimate movie art, by its definition, and which really does not fit into the category of commercial movie art. This gray area is difficult to define in terms of where it fits into the movie art industry, and some consideration should be given before purchasing posters from this area.

The following categories would fit into this gray "quasi-commercial" area. Each is addressed in detail in related articles in the glossary section and the chapter on Foreign Posters.

> Anniversary Issues
> British (See Foreign Posters chapter)
> Cable/Network TV Posters
> International (See Foreign Posters chapter)
> Limited Editions
> Special Issues
> Video Posters

Purchasing Commercial Posters: If the intent of a collector is to purchase a poster that is recognized as "legitimate movie art" by the majority of movie poster collectors that has the potential to increase in value in the collector's market or can be traded to other collectors, then "commercial movie posters" should be avoided. Close scrutiny is required before purchasing posters that fall within one of the categories in the gray "quasi-commercial" area.

See also: Anniversary Issues; Cable/Network TV Posters, Limited Editions; Special Issues; Foreign Posters

Condition

A poster's value as a collectible is determined by a number of factors, one of which is the poster's overall physical condition. Before any value can be assessed, a poster must be analyzed and its condition determined and graded.

Determining Condition/Grading: There are no "carved-in-stone" rules for grading the condition of posters. There are, however, two generalized "grading systems" that are adhered to by most collectors/dealers. There is a third grading system that is used by auction houses. Because there are no set standards, these grading systems are subjective by their nature, and grades can vary among the parties doing the assessing.

In order to arrive at a "grade," the poster must be viewed for any signs of defects or blemishes. These will include such things as: tears, rips, wrinkles, crinkles, creases, missing pieces or chunks, bleedthroughs, marks, stains, tape, fading, writing, etc. The next step is to look at any defects/blemishes in terms of its (their) location in relation to the overall poster. If the defects/blemishes appear in the border of the poster and do not detract from the poster's body or its artwork, the presence of these defects/blemishes generally does not warrant a significantly lower grade. However, if any of these defects/blemishes appear anywhere in the body of the poster, particularly the poster's artwork, they will have a significant effect on the poster's overall grade.

How Grading Affects Pricing: Most movie poster collectors/dealers determine the value of a poster either through their personal knowledge of the current market value of the poster, or by utilizing any of the price guides that are available. Poster prices normally fall within a generally accepted high/low range for its particular title. The high/low range is based solely on the poster's condition. If the poster is given a high grade, it will command top dollar in that title's generally accepted high/low price range. On the other hand, if the poster is in poor condition, it will generally be priced at the lowest end of the title's accepted price range. Simply put, the condition of the poster will determine where within that title's generally accepted price range the value of that particular piece will lie.

Please note, however, that some sellers do not abide by standard pricing guides and set their own prices. It is highly recommended that before purchasing any poster, particularly those of older classics, full market research be conducted to determine if the price is in line with the prices assessed by the majority of collectors/dealers.

Grading Systems: While there are no "written rules" on how to grade a movie poster, there are general guidelines that have generally been adopted by the majority of collectors/dealers throughout the country. The following is the most generally used and accepted grading system.

Grade Condition Factors

Mint: A poster in *mint* condition is one that essentially looks like it just came off of the press. It will have no holes, tears, marks, fading, bleedthroughs or any other defects or blemishes whatsoever. A poster in *mint* condition can be folded or rolled, depending on the manner in which it was originally distributed to the theatres and poster exchanges. A poster in *mint* condition commands top dollar in that title's normal price range.

Near Mint: A poster in *near mint* condition is one that may have small pin holes in the corner, minor wrinkles or small tears in the border only. The artwork is in excellent condition with no blemishes whatsoever. A poster in *near mint* condition commands slightly less than one in *mint* condition.

Very Good: A poster in *very good* condition can have multiple holes or small tears in the border, each measuring up to one inch. There can be some minor fading, or small tears in the artwork along the fold lines only. The poster can also have writing, marks, tape, stain, etc. in the border area. A poster in *very good* condition will command slightly less than one in *near mint* condition.

Good: A poster is in *good* condition if it has tears or small holes that are no larger than a quarter on the outer edges of the poster's artwork. Pieces of the border may be torn or missing; there may be mild bleedthrough in the outer area of the artwork; there may be mild fading. In general, a poster in *good* condition will have minor defects/blemishes around the artwork. The major area of the artwork must be clear of any defects or blemishes. The price of a poster in *good* condition generally falls in the middle to lower end of the price range for that title.

Fair: A poster is considered in *fair* condition if it has major tears, holes, bleedthroughs, stains, fading or other serious defects/blemishes which directly affect the artwork of the poster. The poster is recognizable and the artwork is primarily intact; however, the poster contains one or more of the above defects/ blemishes. The value of a poster in *fair* condition will weigh heavily on its title. If it is a rare piece, it still may command the lower end of the poster's normal price range. A poster in *fair* condition must be professionally restored.

Poor: Posters in *Poor* condition have serious defects such as large tears, large pieces of poster missing, serious fading, or in general, in such poor shape that even the slightest handling adds to the damage. The value of a poster in *poor* condition will weigh heavily on its title. If it is a rare piece, it still may command the lower end of the poster's normal price range. A poster in *poor* condition must be professionally restored.

Some collectors use a slightly different grading system, dividing the grades across nine categories. Auction houses use their own "one letter" grading system. The following scale presents a generalized comparison of the three grading systems:

Auction	6 Grades	9 Grades	
A+	MINT	MINT	
A	NEAR MINT	NEAR MINT	Some
		EXCELLENT	Dealers
B	VERY GOOD	VERY FINE	Classify This
		FINE	Area
B– to C	GOOD	VERY GOOD	As Excellent
		GOOD	
C–	FAIR	FAIR	
POOR	POOR	POOR	

This chart illustrates how the three additional conditions in the nine grading system, Excellent, Very Fine and Fine, would break out if comparing them to the six grade system. For example, if a poster is graded as Excellent, the description of its condition would fall somewhere within the Near Mint to Very Good conditions explained above.

Most auction houses use a "one-letter" grading system. This chart compares this grading system to the standard six grade system. For example, a poster in mint condition would be graded as "A+" by an auction house.

Please remember, however, that each of these grading systems is based solely on the opinion of the appraiser. Conditions will vary from dealer to dealer. The above are simply some general guidelines that are most often used by dealers/collectors in the movie poster industry.

See also: Auctions; Bleedthroughs; Fading; Fair Condition; Folds/Fold Lines; Good Condition; Holes; Linen Backing; Marks; Mint Condition; Near Mint Condition; Poor Condition; Stains; Tears; Trimming; Wrinkles; Very Good Condition

Dead Card

SUMMARY OF FACTS

Size: 8" × 10", 11" × 14".
History: First introduced and distributed in the 1910s.
Purpose: Part of lobby card set.
Current Usage: Lobby cards are issued only in foreign markets.
Notes: The least desirable card in the lobby set.

The dead card is one of the cards that comprise a lobby card set. Lobby sets were initially introduced in the 1910s.

The term "dead card" was coined by movie art collectors to mean the card considered the least desirable in a lobby set. A set of lobby cards typically consists of the following:

- Title Card usually giving credit information (similar to the one sheet) (1 Card)
- Scene cards featuring major stars (2–3 Cards)
- Scene cards featuring minor stars (2–3 Cards)
- Scenery cards featuring large group shots, extras, or just scenery. (Also known as the "**Dead Card**") (1–2 Cards)

Many of the lobby card sets are numbered, showing each card's position in the set (that is, nos. 1–8). The title card is always first, and the dead card is usually numbered later in the series, such as No. 8. The scene cards are numbered in the middle. Prior to the 1960s, the lobby card number was usually found in the corner of the artwork on the card. Post 1960s lobby cards normally have numbers that are printed on the bottom border, in typewriter style.

Current Usage: Lobby sets for American-made films are no longer used in American markets. They are, however, commonly used in foreign movie markets.

Collectibility: Alone, the "dead card" is the item least sought-after by collectors. The exception is the case when the dead would complete a lobby card set. If a collector simply wants a card (any card) from a rare or popular movie, this would be the least expensive card to obtain.

See also: Lobby Cards/Sets; Scene Card; Title Card

Double-Sided Printing

What Are Double-Sided Posters? Starting around the mid–1980s, many of the theatre one sheets were released with both single-sided and double-sided printing. The single-sided posters have printing only on the front, but double-sided posters have artwork on the front and back side. The artwork on the back is the reverse (in lighter shading) of the artwork on the front of the poster. Double-sided posters are normally printed on a thicker paper than the single-sided counterparts.

How the Process Works: The double-sided poster is the result of a very expensive printing process which involves running the initial negative through at normal color intensity. The poster is then reversed and run back through the presses at a reduced color intensity, such as 30 percent to 40 percent of the initial color. This is why the artwork on the front is more colorful and detailed than the reverse print on the back.

What Is the Purpose of Double-Sided Printing? Many theatres throughout the country have a "mirror" display. Because of the reverse artwork on the back, these "mirror" displays give a three-dimensional look to the poster.

There is also the feeling among many collectors that studios began double-sided printing to discourage the unauthorized printing and distributing of movie posters. This, however, is mere speculation.

Collectibility: Double-sided posters are extremely popular with many collectors of newer materials. In fact, some collectors will only collect one sheets that are double-sided. Many collectors of new materials prefer double-sided posters because there is no doubt that the poster is legitimate theatre art. Special edition and anniversary issues are not normally double-sided.

Note: Some video posters are also printed double-sided; however, the back side of the poster is not just a lighter reverse of the front side's artwork. Double-sided video posters are more like two posters put together to make one. The poster may contain two different versions of the artwork for the same movie. There are even some instances where the artwork is from two different movies.

See also: One Sheets; Video Poster

Duotone

Duotone refers to posters and card stock materials which were printed with only two colors (usually black with another color on a white background). There are basically three different categories of duotone movie materials:

- In secondary markets, such as military bases, many major motion picture companies would issue a line of duotone materials in addition to their full color ones for major movie productions. These duotone materials were much less expensive, thereby giving a cheaper alternative for small theatres.
- Major motion picture studios, as well as smaller studios, would issue

materials for low-budget films in duotone, to keep down advertising
costs.
- Because of full color materials were more expensive, a series of secondary printing companies joined the movie advertising market by
introducing a cheaper line of materials, primarily window cards and
heralds, which were printed in duotone.

Duotone materials were initially introduced by major movie studios for
the purpose of providing promotional materials that were less costly to film
exhibitors than the full color posters. They were also a great alternative for cutting advertising costs on low-budget films produced by both major and minor
motion picture studios. The duotone versions of many movie studios' materials were extensively used on American military bases around the world.

Soon, several independent printers introduced a line of primary duotone
window cards as an inexpensive alternative to the National Screen Service
(NSS) materials. These duotone materials were particularly attractive to small
city and rural theatres. Window cards were made for mass distribution, to be
placed in retail and office windows, posted on utility poles, nailed to fences,
etc. As such, many theatres and movie exhibitors found thee duotone window
cards to be extremely cost effective.

Three primary printing companies were known for their duotone window
cards. They are: (1) Benton Card Company; (2) Hatch Card Company; and
(3) Globe Card Company.

The duotone one sheets released by the movie studios through NSS usu-
ally contain the same artwork as their full color counterparts, only in duotone.
They will include the same credit and print information, but will not have the
NSS number or tag line.

The duotone window cards released by the independent printers sometimes contain the same artwork as the NSS window cards, but usually have
their own unique artwork. The name of the printer is normally printed somewhere in the bottom border of the window card.

Collectibility: The value assessed to duotone materials by most movie collectors depends upon which category the materials belong. If a movie studio
released duotone materials along with color versions of the same paper, then
the duotone versions will not command the same dollar value as their color
counterparts. Most collectors prefer the full color over duotone, if both such
versions exist. If, however, the duotone posters are the *only* ones released with
the particular film in question, then the value of these materials would be
based on other factors, such as: How rare or hard to get are the materials? Is
the title popular with collectors? Does the film have a "cult" following? How
old are the materials? In some cases, duotone materials are considered very
valuable, as they are the only such materials that exist for certain movie titles.

Original duotone materials released by independent or secondary printers

Top: Military issue of *Take the High Ground* from military base in South America. Notice there is no NSS tag or NSS number on bottom. *Bottom:* The NSS version was printed in three-color. NSS tag goes across the bottom. NSS number stained but visible.

are generally considered collectible. However, most collectors do not consider them as desirable as the color versions released either through NSS or the movie studios. Even when the artwork and colors are identical, there can be major differences in the prices for materials produced by independent printers and those issued through NSS or the movie studios.

See also: Benton Card Company; National Screen Service; Secondary Printers; Window Card

Fading

Fading is the loss of color and detail in a poster's artwork, resulting in a dull image.

Causes: Fading occurs as the result of a poster being exposed to direct sunlight for long periods of time, such as by being hung in a window.

Effect on Poster's Value: Fading is considered a serious poster defect, and the degree and size of the faded area has a direct impact on the value of the poster. As with all other defects, if the artwork is not damaged and the fading appears on the background or border, the poster's value is not significantly diminished. However, if the colors and graphics of the artwork show signs of fading, then the value of the poster will be affected proportionately.

Repair/Restoration Options: Faded posters can be restored to original color by a professional poster restorer only by repainting the poster.

See also: Condition

Featurette

The term "featurette" is generally applied to any film that is short in duration (not full-length) and is normally shown before a full-length movie presentation. In this context the term can be used to represent any of the following:

Cartoons—Normally up to seven minutes in length
Featurettes—Normally 12–13 minutes in length
Short Subjects—Normally 18–20 minutes in length

Featurette Posters: Occasionally a movie studio will release an individual poster for the featurette. These posters look identical to a theatre one sheet, and normally have a tag somewhere on the poster that indicates the feature movie with which it appeared. Instead of producing an individual poster for a specific featurette, movie studios sometimes opt to put a tag about the featurette on the theatre sheet.

Collectibility: By definition, these posters are legitimate theatre art, as they are issued as advertising materials and distributed directly to the theatres and film exhibitors. In fact, they are very popular with certain movie art collectors, because there are not as many featurettes as there are feature films. This category includes many perennial favorites such as The Three Stooges, Laurel and Hardy, Mickey Mouse, and Roger Rabbit.

See also: Combo Posters

Folds/Fold Lines

Folds/fold lines resulted from pressing, folding or wrinkling paper or card stock materials.

Folds/Fold Lines on Posters/Large Card Stock

Causes: Most pre–1980s materials were folded in order to be mailed to the local movie distributors/exhibitors—thus, most of these materials contain specific fold lines. One sheets were folded in half, then in half again. Some inserts and half sheets were folded in half. Larger sizes were folded down until they were approximately 11" × 14" in size.

Effect on Poster's Value: Because the larger pre–1980 materials were almost always folded for mailing, folds/fold lines are generally acceptable to collectors, and they do not adversely affect the value of the poster. Collectors realize that it is almost impossible to find the larger pre–1980s materials that were not folded at one time. Therefore, folds/fold lines are not considered major defects.

If, however, the folds/fold lines were not the result of folding for mailing purposes, then they are considered a defect in the poster's overall condition and should be assessed according to their size, appearance and location in relation to the poster art.

Folds/Fold Lines on Lobby Cards/Smaller Card Stock

Causes: Folds/fold lines that are found on the smaller card stock materials, particularly lobby cards, are generally the cause of mishandling. Lobby cards were small enough to be mailed to the distributors without being folded, so there is no "acceptable" reason for folds/fold lines.

Window cards were normally sent flat because of their size. However, some distributors folded them in half before mailing. Inserts were generally sent to the theatres rolled, but there were a number of inserts which were folded before being shipped.

Effect on Poster's Value: Folds/fold lines are not acceptable on lobby cards and are considered defects. Their value as a collectible must be assessed accordingly. Even though movie poster distributors did, on occasion, fold the window cards and inserts, the ones that have not been folded are more sought after and therefore command higher prices. Folds/fold lines that are the result of folding for mailing purposes are acceptable, and are not considered major defects in the overall value. Most collectors, however, prefer a nonfolded window card or insert.

Repair/Restoration Options: Fold lines can generally be diminished by carefully following a steaming/drying process. The fold lines are first steamed out by utilizing a heavy-duty clothes steamer. Once the fold lines are moist, a soft clamp is used to anchor one side of the fold line. The other side of the fold line is then gently pulled out. Once the fold has been pulled out, a hair dryer is then used to dry the moist area. Please note that this process may leave a "mark" due to dirt that has accumulated in the fold.

Note that there are dangers in a non-professional attempting this process. It must be done delicately. Once the poster is moist, it can easily be pulled apart if too much pressure is applied. During the drying process, if too much tension is applied, the poster can become warped. The only way to correct a warped poster is through linen backing.

Some poster shops use a heat press to diminish fold lines. These presses work similarly to the devices used by drycleaners to remove wrinkles from clothes.

It is always best to leave any repairs to a professional restorer. However, fold lines can be removed by a layman if the process is followed carefully and the poster is handled delicately.

See also: Condition

40" × 60" Posters

SUMMARY OF FACTS

Size: 40" × 60"; on card stock.

History: First used in the 1930s for certain titles only.

Purpose: Used in theatre lobbies, balconies, and other ad spaces inside and outside theatres, such as bus, train and subway depots, etc.

Current Usage: Very limited current usage.

Notes: Not as commonly used as other paper sizes.

Posters called 40" × 60"s were introduced into the market in the 1930s. They were primarily offered for major motion pictures only. They were used as both inside and outside theatre displays. Their heavy card material made them more durable than paper.

A very heavy card stock material is used for printing 40" × 60"s. The National Screen Service number (NSS) is normally found on the side of the poster, as opposed to the lower bottom as is the case with one sheets. These materials were normally shipped in rolled condition to the theatre exchanges.

Current Usage: These posters have been released for a few selected recent features, but 40" × 60"s are generally issued only in rare instances.

Collectibility: Because of their larger size, they are not as sought-after by the majority of collectors as are the smaller sized posters. However, there are certain collectors that only collect the larger sized posters. They were printed in smaller numbers than were other sizes of advertising materials. Because they normally contained beautiful artwork and were released in smaller numbers, they are in demand by some collectors. Since 40" × 60"s were sent to the exchanges rolled, these materials lose some of their value if they are folded.

See also: Movie Art/Paper

Good Condition

A poster or other size movie paper in "Good" condition is one that can have small holes that are no larger than a quarter on the outer edges of the poster's artwork. Pieces of the border may be torn or missing; there may be mild bleed-through in the outer area of the artwork; there may be mild fading. In general, a poster in "Good" condition will have minor defects and or blemishes around the border and into the outer edges of the artwork. The major area of the artwork must be clear of any defects or blemishes.

Materials in "Good" condition can be folded or rolled, regardless of the manner in which they were originally distributed to the theatres and or poster exchanges.

Value: A price of materials rated in "Good" condition generally falls in the middle to lower end of the price range for that particular movie title.

Comparison to Nine Category Grading System

The following chart shows where a poster in "Good" condition would be placed utilizing the nine category grading system:

6 Grades	9 Grades	
Mint	Mint	
Near Mint	Near Mint	
	Excellent	Some Dealers
Very Good	Very Fine	Classify This
	Fine	Area
Good	Very Good	As Excellent
	Good	
Fair	Fair	
Poor	Poor	

See also: Condition

Half Sheets

SUMMARY OF FACTS

Size: 22" × 28" (horizontal); on card stock.
History: First used in the 1910s.
Purpose: Used for special sized displays.
Current Usage: Discontinued in 1980s.
Notes: Differs from the Jumbo Window Card which measures 22" × 28" vertically; sometimes released in styles A and B.

Half sheets were first introduced in the 1910s, shortly after the one sheet and lobby cards. They were printed on card stock, which made them more versatile than the paper materials. They were initially printed to be used in special sized lobby displays.

Half sheets were initially printed using a brown-and-white rotogravure process (an intaglio printing process using letters and pictures which are transferred from an etched copper cylinder to paper). In the 1920s, studios began producing their card stock materials through a process known as photogelatin/collotype (a printing process utilizing a plate with a gelatin surface carrying the image to be reproduced) or heliotype (a printing process utilizing a photomechanically produced plate for pictures or type made by exposing a gelatin film under a negative, hardening it with chrome aluminum and printing directly from it). This process initially offered one, then two, then three colors. Because the process utilized duller dyes than did lithography (a printing process whereby an image is imprinted on limestone, sheet zinc or aluminum and treated so that it will retain ink, while the non-image area is treated to repel ink—this process was utilized for one sheets and larger paper), the colors of the half sheets look better close up than they do when viewed from a distance.

Half sheets are printed on a lighter card stock material. The artwork on the half sheet may or may not be the same as that of the one sheet. The NSS number is normally found on the lower corner, as is the case with the one sheet, but can also be found on the side.

Half sheets were normally sent to the exhibitors in a rolled condition. However, there were times when they were folded into quarters for mailing. Half sheets were sometimes released in more than one style, such as styles "A" and "B." In some cases the studio would issue one style using photography and one style using painted artwork on the other.

Current Usage: Half sheets were a main tool in the advertising arsenal until the 1980s. Prior to this time, most theatres had just one screen and one feature movie, with the theatre lobbies being covered with various sizes of advertising materials for the one feature presentation (including one sheets, three sheets, half sheets, inserts, 30" × 40"s, 40" × 60"s, and complete lobby card sets). With the advent of multiscreen theatres where as many as twelve movies may be showing simultaneously, the same lobby advertising space had to be divided among all the films being shown. As a consequence of this, movie studios opted to phase out the half sheets, as well as other standard sizes, choosing instead to use one sheets, mini sheets, lobby standups, banners, mobiles, etc.

Collectibility: Half sheets are very popular with collectors, primarily because they are easier to frame. Most collectors prefer half sheets that have never been folded; however, fold marks that were the result of mailing to the exchanges are acceptable. It is quite common to find half sheets in more than one style, such as styles A and B.

See also: Movie Art/Paper; Styles

Heralds

SUMMARY OF FACTS

Size: 5" × 7" or varies; on paper.
History: First used in the 1910s.
Purpose: Used as handbills/flyers.
Current Usage: No longer used.
Notes: Usually included as part of press kit.

Heralds were used as early as the 1910s. Theatre staff would stand on street corners and hand out the heralds to passers-by. The heralds were used as flyers, trying to drum up interest in the film.

Heralds were normally the size of a 5" × 7" or 6" × 9" flyer. Many heralds were larger, and some were more than one page. Printed as an inexpensive ad flyer, the herald normally included a picture of the star or stars and general information about the movie. One herald was normally included in the press kit or campaign kit that was sent to the movie exhibitor. The theatres would take the herald and make copies to be handed out. If the theatre did not want to make the copies, there were several independent printers that were set up to sell the heralds in quantities. These independent printers were usually listed in the press kit.

Current Usage: Heralds were used up until the mid–1960s, particularly for major promotional campaigns.

Collectibility: Heralds are considered collectible but do not command the same dollar value as do the movie's posters. Heralds were distributed by the thousands directly to the public, a fact that lessens their value as a collectible. Conversely, heralds are more affordable, which makes them sought-after by some collectors. Normally heralds are included as part of the press kit, which is also considered collectible.

See also: Movie Art/Paper

Holes in Posters

Causes: Holes are caused by any number of reasons. Pins and staples were sometimes used to display the poster in the theatre lobby. Other holes are the result of mishandling of the poster.

Stored posters can sometimes attract worms and insects such as silverfish.

Effect on Poster's Value: The location and size of the holes will determine what effect, if any, they will have on the overall value of the poster. Holes that are on the border of the poster will not impact the value, generally speaking. However, holes or missing pieces of the poster that are located on the artwork itself is considered a major defect, and will therefore affect the overall value of the poster.

Repair/Restoration Options: If the paper is merely torn back from the poster but is still attached and intact, it can be gently pulled back into place and reattached by use of acid-free archival tape on the back of the poster. The torn piece may be wrinkled, so the wrinkles will have to be gently pulled out before reattaching.

Small pin holes can be repaired by placing acid-free archival tape on the back of the poster and coloring in the front of the tape to match the poster.

Major holes can be restored by a professional poster restorer. Major holes can be repaired in a number of ways, such as filling the hole with a painting material called gesso which is applied and then sanded down, or by linen or paper backing.

See also: Condition

Inserts

SUMMARY OF FACTS

Size: 14" × 36"; on card stock.
History: First used in the 1910s.
Purpose: Used in special sized promotional displays.
Current Usage: Discontinued in early 1980s.
Notes: One of the earliest of movie paper sizes.

Inserts are one of the earliest forms of movie advertising. Introduced shortly after the one sheet in the 1910s, inserts were smaller than the one sheet, and printed on a heavy card stock, which made them more sturdy.

Inserts were initially printed using a brown-and-white rotogravure process (an intaglio printing process using letters and pictures which are transferred from an etched copper cylinder to paper). In the 1920s, studios began producing their card stock materials through a process known as photogelatin/collotype (a printing process utilizing a plate with a gelatin surface carrying the image to be produced) or heliotype (a printing process utilizing a photomechanically produced plate for pictures or type made by exposing a gelatin film under a negative, hardening it with chrome aluminum and printing directly from it). This process initially offered one, then two, then three colors. Because this process utilized duller dyes than did lithography (a printing process whereby an image is imprinted on a limestone, sheet zinc or aluminum and treated so that it will retain ink, while the non-image area is treated to repel ink—this process was utilized for one sheets and larger paper), the colors of the inserts look better close up than they do when viewed from a distance.

Inserts measure 14" × 36" and are printed on a heavier card stock. The artwork on the inserts is most often the same as that issued with the Style A one sheet. Because of their frameable size, they were used through the lobby in special smaller displays.

The inserts were sent to distributors both rolled and folded, so it is not uncommon to acquire inserts in either condition.

Current Usage: Inserts were one of the earliest of advertising tools and were used extensively until the 1980s. Prior to this time, most theatres had just one screen and one feature movie. A lot more advertising attention was given to each movie, with the theatre lobbies being covered with various sizes of advertising materials for the one feature presentation (including one sheets, three sheets, half sheets, inserts, 30" × 40"'s, 40" × 60"'s, and complete lobby card sets). With the advent of multi-screen theatres where as many as twelve movies may be showing simultaneously, the same lobby advertising space had to be divided among all the films being shown. As a consequence of this, movie studios opted to phase out the inserts, as well as other standard sizes, choosing instead to use one sheets, mini sheets, lobby standups, banners, mobiles, etc.

Collectibility: Inserts are extremely popular with collectors for a number of reasons. First, the insert generally has the same artwork as that of the one sheet. Because it is smaller than the one sheet, it is a lot easier to frame and display. Second, the insert is printed on a heavy card stock material, which makes it easier to handle and hard to damage. While it is preferable to have rolled inserts, a folded insert is not uncommon and does not necessarily detract from its value if it was folded when sent initially to the theatres. If an insert was initially sent to theatres in rolled condition, and subsequently folded for some other reason, it can detract from its value.

See also: Movie Art/Paper

Jumbo Lobby Cards

Summary of Facts

Size: 14" × 17"; printed on card stock.
History: First introduced and distributed in 1920s.
Purpose: Used in larger theatre lobby displays.
Current Usage: Today used only in foreign markets.
Notes: They are normally not part of set.

The standard size lobby card represents one of the earliest forms of movie "paper" advertising, dating back to the 1910s. The jumbo lobby card was introduced several years later.

The jumbo lobby card was printed via the processes known as photogelatin/collotype (a printing process utilizing a plate with a gelatin surface carrying the image to be reproduced) or heliotype (a printing process utilizing a photomechanically produced plate for pictures or type made by exposing a gelatin film under a negative, hardening it with chrome aluminum and printing directly from it). These processes initially offered one, then two, then three colors. Because these processes utilized duller dyes than did lithography (a printing process whereby an image is imprinted on a limestone, sheet zinc or aluminum and treated so that it will retain ink, while the non-image area is treated to repel ink—this process was utilized for one sheets and larger paper), the colors of the lobby cards look better close up than they do when viewed from a distance.

A jumbo lobby card measures 14" × 17" and usually depicts a scene from the movie. It is printed on card stock material and displayed in and around the lobbies of theatres. Unlike the standard and mini lobby cards, jumbo lobby cards are generally not part of a set.

Current Usage: Lobby cards were a main advertising tool until the 1980s. Prior to this time, most theatres had just one screen and one feature movie. A lot more advertising attention was given to each movie, with the theatre lobbies being covered with various sizes of advertising materials for the one feature presentation (including one sheets, three sheets, half sheets, 30" × 40"s, 40" × 60"s, and complete lobby card sets. With the advent of multi-screen theatres where as many as twelve movies may be showing simultaneously, the same lobby advertising space had to be divided among all the films being shown. As a consequence of this, movie studios opted to phase out the lobby card sets, as well as other standard sizes, choosing instead to use one sheets, mini sheets, lobby standups, banners, mobiles, etc.

Theatres throughout Europe, and other countries around the world, however, continue to use lobby cards in their theatres. Consequently, American movie studios will print lobby cards for distribution to the European theatre market.

Collectibility: Because of their "frameable" size and their history, lobby cards are very popular with movie art collectors.

See also: Lobby Cards/Sets; Movie Art/Paper

Jumbo Window Cards

SUMMARY OF FACTS

Size: 22" × 28" (vertical); on card stock.
History: First used in the 1910s.
Purpose: Used for special sized displays.
Current Usage: No longer used.
Notes: Differs from the half-sheet which measures 22" × 28" horizontally.

Window cards were first introduced in the 1910s, shortly after the one sheet and lobby cards. Window cards were produced in three sizes—standard, jumbo and mini.

Window cards were printed on cheaper card stock, which made them more versatile than the paper materials. They were initially printed in large numbers so that they could be placed in windows of stores, barber shops, beauty shops, doctor and dental offices, bakeries, in and around a community.

Jumbo window cards were initially printed using a brown-and-white rotogravure process. (An intaglio printing process using letters and pictures which are transferred from an etched copper cylinder to paper). In the 1920s, studios began producing their card stock materials through a process known as photogelatin/collotype (a printing process utilizing a plate with a gelatin surface carrying the image to be reproduced) or heliotype (a printing process utilizing a photomechanically produced plate for pictures or type made by exposing a gelatin film under a negative, hardening it with chrome aluminum and printing directly from it). This process initially offered one, later two, then three colors.

Because this process utilized duller dyes than did lithography (a printing process whereby an image is imprinted on limestone, sheet zinc or aluminum and treated so that it will retain ink, while the non-image area is treated to repel ink—this process was utilized for one sheets and larger paper), the colors of the jumbo window cards look better close up than they do when viewed from a distance.

Jumbo window cards are printed on a heavier, cheaper card stock material. The artwork on the jumbo window card may or may not be the same as that of the one sheet. These jumbo window cards have a top border of four to six inches which is left blank. This was used by the theatre to write in the dates and show times of the featured film. Sometimes the theatres would staple paper banners with the theatre's name on this blank area.

Jumbo window cards were normally shipped to the theatre and film exhibitors flat. Since they were normally not originally folded, jumbo window cards lose their value if they contain fold lines or creases.

Current usage: Jumbo window cards are no longer used by major studios. This size was discontinued in the 1980s along with a number of other popular sizes. This is partially due to the growing trend toward suburban shopping malls and the studios' attempts to reduce advertising expenses.

Collectibility: Because jumbo window cards were produced in larger quantities, they are not considered as valuable as other sizes, such as one sheets and two sheets. However, this size window card was not as common as the regular size window card, so there are not as many of this sized window card on the market. Their numbers would fall somewhere in between the regular window cards and the one sheets. They are, however, popular with some collectors because of their frameable size and because they are cheaper to obtain than other materials from the same time period.

See also: Half Sheets; Midget Window Cards; Window Cards

Jumbo window card is 22" × 28" like half sheet but is vertical instead of horizontal.

Kilian Enterprises

Jeff Kilian, founder of Kilian Enterprises, received permission from Lucasfilm Ltd. to put out a special issue of the *L'Affiche Movie Poster Collector's Newsletter* including all of the *Star Wars Saga* American movie posters. In 1985, Kilian released the *Star Wars Saga* American One Sheet Poster Checklist, which has become known to collectors as the *Star Wars "Poster of Posters,"* because it has pictures and information on every American one sheet that was printed for *Star Wars* and its sequel movies up to that date.

Jessica gold mylar is tagged Style E of *Who Framed Roger Rabbit?* Kilian Enterprises produced poster with Dayna Stedry's artwork. Symbol is actually her birthday.

Special issue of *Return of the Jedi*; only received by fan club members. Notice fan club stamp which was stamped in gold. Advance tenth anniversary poster with *Revenge of the Jedi* artwork.

Because of the popularity of this poster, Kilian Enterprises started on a course of creating, producing and issuing a variety of anniversary and special edition posters. These included anniversary issues for the *Star Wars* series, *Indiana Jones*, *Alien*, and *The Day the Earth Stood Still*. They also issued special edition posters for *Who Framed Roger Rabbit?*, including two gold mylar posters of "Jessica Rabbit" and the set of commemoratives.

Kilian's posters are unlike other anniversary or special edition posters because of their unique and beautiful artwork. Some of the artwork on Kilian's posters is designed by Dayna Stedry (Mrs. Kilian). Kilian also used artwork from other well-known commercial artists, such as Drew, Alvin, and Rodriguez for some of his projects.

Kilian's posters are normally one sheet size and carry the tag "Kilian Enterprises" somewhere in the bottom border.

Collectibility: Because Kilian sets a high standard of artwork and beauty in creating a unique piece, his posters are accepted even by some of the most conservative movie art collectors. Kilian's posters are individually numbered, which adds to the collectibility.

See also: Anniversary Issues; Limited Editions; Special Issues

Limited Editions

The term "limited edition" was first introduced in the art world. Original pieces of art are expensive and rare, so reproductions were made in limited numbers to be offered to the public. These "limited editions" were normally of high quality and individually numbered.

Limited editions followed in animation art, where original seriographs were copied and released in limited numbers to collectors. In recent years, "limited editions" have been introduced to the movie art industry.

Limited edition movie posters generally meet the following criteria:

- Contain original artwork
- Released in limited numbers
- Meant to be sold to the public
- Are issued or authorized by movie studios

In addition, better quality limited editions are individually numbered.

The classification of limited edition movie art would include anniversary issues, commemoratives and special issues, such as those printed on mylar.

Who Issues Limited Editions: In addition to individual movie studios who, from time to time, issue limited editions on some of their classics, there are a number of independent companies who get the permission of the studios to release certain limited edition movie posters. While there are a number of independents, the two most recognized are as follows:

Tenth anniversary issue of *Return of the Jedi* was done by Kazo Sano. Artwork was done for original release but came in second in an art contest for George Lucas.

- **Kilian Enterprises:** Kilian Enterprises is an independent printer who has issued some of the most beautiful and sought after limited edition posters including those for *Star Wars, Indiana Jones, Who Framed Roger Rabbit?, Alien, The Day the Earth Stood Still,* and others. Kilian creates its own artwork, or uses well-known established poster artists to create new artwork, with the approval of the studio. The posters issued by Kilian are individually numbered. Because their posters present new artwork, even many conservative collectors accept these posters as collectible because they contain artwork not available on any other poster.
- **Suncoast Motion Picture Company:** Suncoast Motion Picture Company, a Division of the Musicland Group, has retail outlets in shopping malls throughout the country. Unlike Kilian, they do not utilize different artwork. They contract with certain movie studios for permission to print 5,000 copies of the studio's movie poster. This classifies such a printing as a limited edition. However, because the artwork is the same as that on the theatre sheet, most collectors do not accept them as collectibles and consider them closer to commercial than to a movie art collectible.

See also: Commercial Posters; Kilian Enterprises; Special Issues; Suncoast Movie Company

Linen Backing

Linen backing is a double mounting process whereby a poster is mounted to cloth, such as linen or cotton. Linen backing helps preserve the poster; makes the poster more durable; and is used by professional restorers to repair posters and return them to their original condition.

When the process was first utilized for movie posters, real linen was used as the backing cloth. Linen is extremely beautiful, soft, pliable and expensive. Most of today's restorers use 100 percent cotton duck. Cotton duck is a canvas material which is stiffer than linen, but is about one-third the cost. Linen is still used on occasion for extremely rare pieces.

The Process: Proper linen backing is actually accomplished through a double mounting process—first putting the poster on a sheet of acid-free Japanese rice paper, then mounting the poster (with the rice paper) onto the duck clock.

Sometimes a poster is mounted directly on to the cloth to keep the mounting cost down. This type of mounting is not recommended because:

1. The poster does not stick as well to cloth as it does to paper;
2. Because of temperature extremes and moisture, or lack of moisture, paper shrinks and moves differently from cloth. Because of the constant

friction between the paper and cloth over time, lines will form in the paper and the poster will begin to disintegrate.

It is more desirable to mount paper to paper than paper to cloth. The rice paper acts as a neutralizer between the paper and cloth.

Impact on Poster's Value: Posters that are linen backed for preservation purposes and are in very good or better condition normally command slightly higher dollars than their unbacked counterparts. If, however, a poster is linen-backed for restoration purposes, the value of the poster could jump significantly, depending on the poster. For example, a poster that normally sells for $1,000 in mint condition would sell for only a fraction of that amount in poor condition. By having it professionally restored and linen backed, the value of the poster would increase to the $1,000 market value.

Linen backing is normally done on one sheets and other paper posters. Paper backing is suggested for card stock materials.

Note: Be aware that sometimes linen backing is done to hide the back of a poster which may indicate that the poster is either a counterfeit or possibly poorly restored.

Lobby Cards/Sets

SUMMARY OF FACTS

Size: 11" × 14" (standard), 8" × 10" (mini), and 14" × 17" (jumbo), on card stock.

History: First introduced and distributed in 1910s.

Purpose: Used in theatre lobbies.

Current Usage: Today used only in foreign markets.

Notes: One of the oldest forms of movie paper.

Lobby cards represent one of the earliest forms of movie "paper" advertising, dating back to the 1910s. The first lobby cards were actually 8" × 10" black and white stills, which were soon replaced with color lobby cards. The color lobby cards were initially printed using a brown-and-white rotogravure process (an intaglio printing process using letters and pictures which are transferred from an etched copper cylinder to paper). Some of the cards were colored in by hand using a stencil. These non-shaded hand painted colors are a direct contrast to the half tones of brown and white which were created by this printing process.

In the 1920s Paramount Studios produced their lobby cards utilizing an offset image process which applied color cut outs to white card stock. At the same time, other studios began producing their cards through a process known as photogelatin/collotype (a printing process utilizing a plate with a gelatin surface carrying the image to be reproduced) or heliotype (a printing process utilizing a photomechanically produced plate for pictures or type made by exposing a gelatin film under a negative, hardening it with chrome aluminum and printing directly from it). This process initially offered one, later two, then three colors. Because this process utilized duller dyes than did lithography (a printing process whereby an image is imprinted on limestone, sheet zinc or aluminum and treated so that it will retain ink, while the non-image area is treated to repel ink—this process was utilized for one sheets and larger paper), the colors of the lobby cards look better close up than they do when viewed from a distance.

A lobby card is essentially what its name implies. Lobby cards depict various scenes from a movie printed on card stock material and displayed in and around the lobbies of theatres—thus the name "lobby card."

Lobby cards usually come in one of these sizes:

- Standard—measuring 11" × 14"
- Mini—measuring 8" × 10"
- Jumbo—measuring 14" × 17"

Lobby cards were printed and issued to the movie theatres in sets. The average lobby set consists of eight different cards. Some lobby card sets contain as many as 16 or more different cards. One of the purposes of lobby cards was to give a pictorial synopsis of the subject movie.

A typical lobby card set consists of the following:

- Title card usually giving credit information (similar to the one sheet) (1 card)
- Scene cards featuring major stars (2–3 cards)
- Scene cards featuring minor stars (2–3 cards)
- Scenery cards featuring large group shots, extras, or just scenery (also known as the "Dead Card") (1–2 cards)

Exception: Paramount Studios never issued title cards in their lobby card sets.

Many of the lobby card sets are numbered, showing each card's position in the set (that is, 1–8). The title card is always first, and the dead card is usually numbered later in the series, such as No. 8. Prior to the 1960s, the lobby card number was usually found in the corner of the artwork on the card. Post 1960s lobby cards normally have numbers that are printed on the bottom border, in typewriter style.

Current Usage: Lobby cards were a main advertising tool until the 1980s. Prior to this time, most theatres had just one screen and one feature movie. A lot more advertising attention was given to each movie, with the theatre lobbies being covered with various sizes of advertising materials for the one feature

Most lobby cards have a number from 1 to 8 on the bottom but some older cards may have the number in the corner of the artwork or not at all.

presentation (including one sheets, three sheets, half sheets, 30 × 40s, 40 × 60s, and complete lobby card sets. With the advent of multi-screen theatres where as many as twelve movies may be showing simultaneously, the same lobby advertising space had to be divided among all the films being shown. As a consequence of this, movie studios opted to phase out the lobby card sets, as well as other standard sizes, choosing instead to use one sheets, mini sheets, lobby standups, banners, mobiles, etc.

Theatres throughout Europe, Mexico, South America and various countries around the world, however, continue to use lobby cards in their theatres. Consequently, American movie studios will print lobby card sets for distribution to the European theatre market.

Collectibility: Because of their frameable size and their history, lobby cards are very popular with movie art collectors. The most popular of these cards among collectors is the first or "title" card. The lobby cards containing scenes of major stars are also sought-after. The minor stars scene cards are next in line as far as collectibility, with scenery cards (dead cards) being the least desirable. In most cases, the minor star scene and scenery cards are sought by collectors just to complete a lobby set.

Because the newer lobby cards are still very popular with many collectors (Disney lobby sets are especially sought after), European lobby cards are being brought back to the United States for collectors, and these are becoming increasingly popular.

See also: Dead Card; Jumbo Lobby Cards; Mini Lobby Cards/Sets; Movie Art/Paper; Scene Cards

Marks

A mark is defined as any blemish on the front of the poster which is caused by pens, markers, grease pencils, regular pencils, crayons, or any other type of writing device.

Most marks found on posters were put there intentionally. Mustaches and devil's horns may be found on the faces of leading men and ladies. Scribble marks, doodles and other "color additions" at the hands of amateur artists can be found on posters.

Effect on Poster's Value: Marks that are present on the border of a poster do not impact the value. Marks of any kind that deface the artwork of the poster are considered serious blemishes and will severely affect the poster's value. Marks that are located on the back of the poster are not considered a defect, unless they result in a bleed-through that can be seen on the front.

Repair/Restoration Options: There are a number of options to repairing marks on posters, depending on whether the marks are old or new.

If the mark is the result of an older fountain pen, an ink eradicator can be used to remove the mark. Ink eradicator is a type of bleach, so when the mark is removed, so is the color on the poster. Thus, the area where the ink eradicator is applied would have to be colored in.

If the mark is the result of indelible ink or newer ball point pens, it cannot be bleached out. *These marks would have to be removed by a professional restorer.*

Pencil marks can be removed with the use of a yellow brick art gum eraser. The art gum eraser is very soft and crumbly. Regular pen and pencil erasers will remove not only the mark, but also all color. *A regular pen or pencil eraser should never be used to remove any type of marks.*

Since removing marks from the artwork of a poster almost always results in the loss of color, *it is highly recommended that the removal of such stains be done by a professional poster restorer only.*

See also: Condition

Midget Window Cards

SUMMARY OF FACTS

Size: 8" × 14" (untrimmed); on card stock.
History: First used in the 1930s.
Purpose: Used primarily as counter and window displays.
Current Usage: Discontinued in 1940s.
Notes: Also known as "mini" window cards.

Window cards were first introduced in the 1910s, shortly after the one sheet and lobby cards. Midget window cards were introduced around the 1930s as a smaller version of the standard size window cards.

Window cards were printed on cheaper card stock, which made them more versatile than the paper materials. They were initially printed in large numbers so that they could be placed in windows of stores, barber shops, beauty salons, doctor and dental offices, bakeries, and on poles in and around a community.

Midget window cards were initially printed using a brown-and-white rotogravure process (an intaglio printing process using letters and pictures which are transferred from an etched copper cylinder to paper). In the 1920s, studios began producing their card stock materials through a process known as photo-gelatin/collotype (a printing process utilizing a plate with a gelatin surface carrying the image to be reproduced) or heliotype (a printing process using a photomechanically produced plate for pictures or type made by exposing a gelatin film under a negative, hardening it with chrome aluminum and printing directly from it). This process initially offered one, later two, then three colors.

Because this process utilized duller dyes than did lithography (a printing process whereby an image is imprinted on limestone, sheet zinc or aluminum and treated so that it will retain ink, while the non-image area is treated to repel ink—this process was utilized for one sheets and larger paper), the colors of the midget window cards look better close up than they do when viewed from a distance.

Midget window cards are printed on a heavier, cheaper card stock material. The artwork on the midget window card may or may not be the same as that of the one sheet. These midget window cards have a top border of 3" to 4" inches which are left blank. This was used by the theatre to write in the dates and show times of the featured film. Sometimes the theatres would staple paper banners with the theatre's name in this blank area.

Midget window cards were normally shipped to the theatre and film exhibitors flat. Since they normally were not originally folded, midget window cards lose their value if they contain fold lines or creases.

Current Usage: Midget window cards were used primarily during the 1930s to 1940s for major motion pictures only. They are no longer used in today's market.

Collectibility: Because midget window cards were produced in large quantities, they are not considered as valuable as other sizes, such as one sheets and two sheets, to most collectors. They were not, however, as common as the regular size window cards, so there are fewer of this size on the market. They are, however, popular with some collectors because of their frameable size and because they are cheaper to obtain than other materials from the same time period.

See also: Half Sheets; Jumbo Window Cards; Movie Art/Paper; Window Cards

Mini Lobby Cards/Sets

SUMMARY OF FACTS

Size: 8" × 10"; on card stock.
History: First introduced and distributed in 1930s.
Purpose: Used in theatre lobbies.
Current Usage: Used in foreign markets.
Notes: Produced in lobby sets.

Even though the first "lobby cards" released in the 1910s were 8" × 10" black and white stills, they were considered, at one time, to be standard sized lobby cards. The "mini lobby cards," as they are known today, were first introduced in the 1930s and measure 8" × 10". They were offered an alternative smaller size.

These mini lobby cards were produced through a process known as photogelatin/collotype (a printing process utilizing a plate with a gelatin surface carrying the image to be reproduced) or heliotype (a printing process utilizing a photomechanically produced plate for pictures or type made by exposing a gelatin film under a negative, hardening it with chrome aluminum and printing directly from it). This process initially offered one, later two, then three colors. Because this process utilized duller dyes than did lithography (a printing process whereby an image is imprinted on limestone, sheet zinc or aluminum and treated so that it will retain ink, while the non-image area is treated to repel ink—this process was utilized for one sheets and larger paper), the colors of the lobby cards look better close up than they do when viewed from a distance.

Mini lobby cards depict various scenes from a movie printed on card stock material and displayed in and around the lobbies of theatres.

Mini lobby cards were printed and issued to the movie theatres in sets. The average mini lobby set consists of eight different cards. Some mini lobby card sets contain as many as 16 or more different cards. One of the purposes of lobby cards was to give a pictorial synopsis of the subject movie.

A typical lobby card set consists of the following:

- Title card usually giving credit information (similar to the one sheet) (1 card)
- Scene cards featuring major stars (2–3 cards)
- Scene cards featuring minor stars (2–3 cards)
- Scenery cards featuring large group shots, extras, or just scenery. (Also known as the "Dead Card") (1–2 cards)

Exception: Paramount Studios never issued title cards in their lobby card sets.

Many of the mini lobby card sets are numbered, showing each card's position in the set (that is, 1–8). The title card is always first, and the dead card is usually numbered later in the series, such as No. 8. Prior to the 1960s, the lobby card number was usually found in the corner of the artwork on the card. Post 1960s mini lobby cards normally have numbers that are printed on the bottom border, in typewriter style.

Current Usage: Mini lobby cards were a main advertising tool until the 1980s. Prior to this time, most theatres had just one screen and one feature movie. A lot more advertising attention was given to each movie, with the theatre lobbies being covered with various sizes of advertising materials for the one feature presentation (including one sheets, three sheets, half sheets, 30" × 40"s, 40" × 60"s, and complete lobby card sets. With the advent of multi-screen theatres where as many as twelve movies may be showing simultaneously, the same lobby advertising space had to be divided among all the films being shown. As a consequence of this, movie studios opted to phase out the mini lobby card sets, as well as other standard sizes, choosing instead to use one sheets, mini sheets, lobby standups, banners, and mobiles.

Theatres throughout Europe, Mexico, South America and various countries around the world, however, continue to use mini lobby cards in their theatres. Consequently, American movie studios will print mini lobby card sets for distribution to the European theatre market.

Collectibility: Because of their frameable size and their history, mini lobby cards are very popular with movie art collectors. The most popular of these lobby cards among collectors is the first or "title" card. The mini lobby cards containing scenes of major stars are also sought-after. The minor stars scene cards are next in line as far as collectibility, with scenery cards (dead cards) being the least desirable. In most cases, the minor star scene and scenery cards are sought by collectors just to complete a lobby set.

Because the newer mini lobby cards are still very popular with many collectors (Disney lobby sets are especially sought-after), European lobby cards are being brought back to the United States for collectors, and these are becoming increasingly popular.

See also: Dead Card; Jumbo Lobby Cards; Lobby Cards/Sets; Movie Art/Paper; Scene Cards

Mini-Sheets

SUMMARY OF FACTS

Size: Varies; on paper.
History: Recently introduced.

Purpose: Lobby displays, giveaways, special promotions.
Current Usage: Widely used.
Notes: Sometimes used as giveaways similar to heralds of old.

Mini sheets primarily came about with the decline of the National Screen Service. At that time, most major motion picture studios began controlling their paper advertising materials. Old movie advertising standards such as the insert, window card and half sheet were no longer useful in the new multi-screen theatres. In their place, studios have chosen to supplement their use of one sheets with new advertising tools, including the mini sheet.

As its name implies, the "mini sheet" is simply a small poster, printed on poster paper. They come in a variety of sizes, depending on the studio and the film. In many cases, the mini sheet is an exact duplicate of the one sheet, only smaller. The size of mini sheets can range from that of a half sheet down to almost that of a herald, depending on the purposes outlined by the studio. Quite often, mini sheets are printed as advances to help generate interest in the film.

Usage: While the mini sheet can be displayed in the lobby, it is most often used in connection with special promotions or giveaways. Mini sheets are frequently given away at movie premieres or special screenings. They are used in the same way as the heralds were at one time.

Collectibility: Although the popularity of mini sheets will never compete with that of inserts, half sheets and window cards of old, they are gaining favor with some new collectors because of their small, frameable size and colorful artwork.

See also: Half Sheets; Heralds; Inserts; Movie Art/Paper; National Screen Service; One Sheet; Window Cards

Mint Condition

What Is Meant by "Mint" Condition? A poster or other size movie paper in "Mint" condition is one that essentially looks like it just came off of the press. It will have no holes, tears, marks, fading, bleedthroughs or any other defects or blemishes whatsoever.

Depending on the size and type of the movie art, materials in "Mint" condition can be folded or rolled, depending on the manner in which they were originally distributed to the theatres and poster exchanges. If the poster/movie paper was initially distributed in a folded condition, as was the case with most large paper sizes that are dated before 1980s (including one sheets, two sheets, three sheets, six sheets, 24 sheets, etc.), fold lines that are present due to the poster being folded for shipping will not detract from its "Mint" condition rating. However, if the poster was folded, or has fold lines not associated with folding it for distribution, then the poster would not be graded as "Mint." In addition, smaller card stock materials, such as lobby cards and window cards, were never folded. As such, a lobby card/window card considered in "Mint" condition cannot have fold lines. Sizes such as inserts and half sheets were, on occasion, folded by the studio/distributor. If this is the case, then fold lines would not detract from a "Mint" rating. However, if the fold lines are the result of some other type of folding, then the item would not be considered in "Mint" condition.

Value: A poster in "Mint" condition commands top dollar for that title's standard retail price range.

Comparison to Nine Category Grading System: The following chart shows where a poster in "Mint" condition would be placed utilizing the nine category grading system:

See also: Condition

6 Grades	9 Grades	
Mint	Mint	
Near Mint	Near Mint	
Near Mint	Excellent	Some Dealers
Very Good	Very Fine	Classify This
Very Good	Fine	Area As
Good	Very Good	Excellent
Good	Good	
Fair	Fair	
Poor	Poor	
Poor		

Movie Art/Paper

The terms "movie art" and "movie paper" are interchangeably used to refer to the advertising materials that are released by movie studios as part of their overall promotional campaign for a movie. These materials are used in a variety of ways, including theatre lobby displays, newspaper and magazine advertising, bus and train depot advertising, billboard advertising, special promotions, special screenings, etc. Movie advertising materials are printed and distributed to *movie theatres or film exhibitors and are not intended for public dissemination.* This one point distinguishes "legitimate" movie art or movie paper from those movie-related products that are produced commercially for direct sale to the public.

From the very beginning, American movie studios recognized the importance of using advertising materials for the successful promotion of their films. In 1909, Thomas Edison, whose Motion Pictures Patents Company consisted of some of the biggest American movie studios operating at that time, organized the General Film Company for the purpose of distributing the films produced by their member studios. In an effort to "standardize" the types and forms of advertising materials to be used in promoting their films, the General Film Company (through Thomas Edison) introduced the "one sheet" poster, which measured 27" × 41". In order to ensure conformity, they contracted with A. B. See Lithograph Company of Cleveland, Ohio, to print them.

As the movie industry grew, other standardized advertising materials were introduced. Soon a typical advertising package could include materials ranging from mini lobby cards to billboard sized posters.

Through the years, forces inside and outside of the movie industry brought about changes in the advertising material lineup. Paper shortages during World War II, the introduction of television advertising, and the trend toward multi-screen theatres were just a few of the events that led to the introduction of new materials and the elimination of others. Today's movie studios use very few of the "old standards" that were once the foundation of a film's advertising program. However, to the delight of most movie art collectors, the one sheet is still widely used and going strong.

Advertising Materials Breakdown: After the introduction of the one sheet in 1909, a number of other "standardized" items followed, each with a specific area of advertising in mind. Through the years, as the movie industry and the world around it changed, many of the products were discontinued, and newer materials were added in their place.

The following chart describes the most commonly used standardized items, terms that are prevalent throughout the movie poster collecting industry. The sizes referenced apply to the American market. Sizes in the foreign markets vary by country. (See chapter on Foreign Posters.) There were times when a studio would introduce special promotional materials for specific films. However, the majority of movie studios used most or all of these materials at one time or another. The charts are broken down by "paper" (products printed on paper), "card stock" (products that are printed on various types of cardboard), and "promotional materials" (products printed on both paper and card stock but taking very unique forms).

Paper Materials

Product	Size	Intended Use	Current Status
One Sheet	27" × 41" (or 27" × 40" after 1980s)	Theatre lobbies; theatre marquees; glass display cases; balconies and ad spaces in and around the theatres (bus, train, subway depots, etc.)	Widely used today.
2 Sheet/ Subway	41" × 81"	Subway advertising.	Used in subways.
3 Sheet	81" × 81"	Larger lobby displays.	Rarely used today.
6 Sheet		Small billboards.	Rarely used today.
24 Sheet		Large billboards.	Rarely used today.
Mini	Varies	Promotions, giveaways, small ad space areas.	Widely used.

Card Stock Materials

Product	Size	Intended Use	Current Status
Lobby Cards			
Mini	8" × 10" or 8" × 14"	Theatre lobbies	Used in foreign markets.
Standard	11" × 14"	Theatre lobbies.	Used in foreign markets.
Jumbo	14" × 17"	Theatre lobbies.	Used in foreign markets.
Inserts	14" × 36"	Small and large theatre lobbies; outside the- atres in small ad space.	No longer used.
Half-Sheet	22" × 28"	Special displays.	Rarely used.
Window Card			
Jumbo	22" × 28" (Vertical)	Window displays in stores, barber shops, bakeries, restaurants; small and rural cities.	No longer used.
Standard	14" × 22"	Same as above.	No longer used.
Mini	10" × 18"	Same as above.	No longer used.
30" × 40"	30" × 40"	Special displays.	No longer used.
40" × 60"	40" × 60"	Special displays.	No longer used

Promotion Materials

Product	Size	Intended Use	Current Status
Ad Slicks/ Sheets	Varies.	Newspaper advertising.	Widely used today.
Campaign Book	Varies.	Full promotional program for use by theatres including newspaper, TV and radio ad campaigns; buttons, giveaways, ideas for special promotions, camera-ready ads, etc.	No longer used. Today's version is called Press Kit.
Heralds	Varies.	Handouts to theatre-goers, passers-by on the streets.	No longer used.
Press Kit	Varies.	Full press program for use by theatres; typically includes newspaper, TV and radio ad campaigns; camera-ready ads, slicks, press stills, slides, buttons, giveaways, etc.	Widely used today.
Programs	Varies; usually leaflet style.	Handout to moviegoers as souvenirs; gives credit info. Only	Rarely used.

		used for major motion pictures. Some programs were sold and not given free.	
Scene Stills	8" × 10" B&W or color	Used for newspaper, magazine and other printed media; part of press kit/ campaign book.	Widely used.
Banners	Varies; printed on vinyl/canvas	Used inside or outside of theatres in large ad area.	Widely used for major productions—A grade movies.
Standees	Varies; normally life-sized or larger	Used as floor display inside theatre lobbies.	Widely used for major productions—A grade movies.
Mobiles	Varies	Used as ceiling display inside theatre lobbies.	Widely used for major productions—A grade movies.

The foregoing chart is not all-inclusive; other items were used from time to time in theatre promotions. However, this chart covers the most common items that are available to movie poster collectors.

See also: See individual articles throughout reference section.

National Screen Service

The National Screen Service was created in 1920 for the purpose of producing and distributing movie "trailers," which had, up to this point in time, been handled by the movie studios themselves. The trailers, which consisted of scenes of coming attractions shown after the feature presentation (thus, the name "trailer"), were an integral part of a studio's overall advertising campaign.

The NSS contracted with several of the larger motion picture companies, including United Artists, Loew's and Columbia, to handle the production and distribution of all of their movie trailers.

The creation and distribution of the "movie paper" or "standard accessories," as they were known in the industry, remained within the control of the movie studios themselves. Because the theatres or film exhibitors had to deal with each studio individually for the "movie paper," a number of independent "exhibitor exchanges" came into existence. These independent exhibitor exchanges basically operated as movie paper "jobbers," creating one place for theatres to go to get their movie paper advertising supplies.

Because of the costs involved in maintaining a "movie paper" department, Paramount Pictures approached the NSS in 1939 about taking over the handling of their movie paper activities. This movie paper included 8" × 10" stills, lobby cards, half sheets, inserts, one sheets, three sheets, six sheets and twenty four sheets. Additional accessories of various sizes were also included in this group. Paramount and NSS entered into an exclusive five-year license on December 22, 1939. This contract was later extended by letter agreement until December 31, 1949. This contract required National Screen to: (1) maintain local branches in each city where Paramount had a film exchange; (2) open the new offices and staff them at their own expense; (3) manufacture and distribute a full line of standard accessories for Paramount movies; and (4) purchase Paramount's existing inventory of standard accessories.

RKO, which had also suffered losses from its accessories business, was approached by NSS about taking over the distribution of their movie paper. On January 31, 1940, RKO entered into an exclusive five-year contract with Advertising Accessories, Inc., the affiliate of National Screen Service, to manufacture and distribute a full line of standard accessories. This contract was later extended to January 31, 1950, by a supplemental agreement dated October 6, 1944.

In 1940, Advertising Accessories also approached Universal Studios and Columbia, but they could not reach an agreement with either studio. They did, however, sign a one-year non-exclusive license agreement for the distribution of Warner Bros.' movie paper on September 26, 1940. This agreement was extended by a letter agreement for successive yearly periods up to and including August 31, 1945.

Columbia, Loew's, Fox, United Artists, Universal and Warner studios utilized the services of regional exhibitor exchanges, rather than NSS, to distribute the standard accessories that they produced for their movies.

In 1940, NSS began renting standard accessories for pictures of other film producers which they obtained from regional exhibitor exchanges. On July 18, 1941, Advertising Accessories, Inc., merged with National Screen Service. In 1941, NSS began negotiating a manufacturing and distributing contract with Loew's. By this time, Loew's too had been experiencing losses in this phase of their business. On February 6, 1942, Loew's and NSS entered into a ten-year exclusive contract. Under this contract, Loew's agreed to furnish to NSS the completed artwork and still negatives from which the mats would be prepared.

Over the next few years, the remainder of the eight major studios at the time signed contacts giving exclusive rights to the National Screen Service to produce and distribute all of the movie paper and standard accessories for their films. Universal signed their contract in 1944, Columbia Pictures in 1945, United Artists in 1946 and 20th Century–Fox in 1947. Warner Bros., who had signed a non-exclusive contract earlier, gave exclusive rights to produce and distribute their movie paper to NSS in 1946.

How Did NSS Operate? With a few exceptions, the advertising materials were sent to the National Screen Service by the studios. The NSS then produced, printed, distributed and stocked all of the materials.

National Screen Services had regional offices set up throughout the United States. In 1943, NSS subcontracted with a number of independent exhibitor exchanges throughout the country. These independent exhibitor exchanges would get their movie paper from NSS and distribute or rent them directly to theatres. Theatre owners would simply come to one of the NSS offices or one of the independent subcontractors to get their advertising materials. If the materials were rented, they would be returned after use for credit toward other advertising materials.

The NSS Numbering System: In an effort to control the number of materials going through, the NSS instituted a date and code system. The NSS had regional offices set up throughout the country. All movie materials distributed through the National Screen Service bear the NSS number.

The NSS number is found on the lower right of the poster. Prior to and including part of the year 1977, the NSS number consisted of two digits, then a slash (/), and one to four digits. The first two digits indicated the year of release, the slash was a divider, and the last four digits represented the sequential order of the movie for that year. For example, an NSS number of 69/22 indicated that the movie was released in 1969, and was the 22nd movie title coded by NSS for the year 1969.

The NSS changed their numbering system during 1977. The same numeric breakdown was used, but the slash (/) was eliminated. The first two digits of the number represent the year the poster is released. The last digits represent the sequential order of the release for the particular year.

In order to indicate a poster is a rerelease or reissue, all NSS numbers contain the letter "R" preceding the number code. Any NSS number containing an "R" in the first position indicates that the poster was released or reissued in the year indicated.

The NSS Tag: In addition to the NSS number, the National Screen Service also included a tag across the bottom of the poster. Although the language

77/42 **770175**

#23
"THE SPY WHO LOVED ME"

'GRAYEAGLE'

In 1977 the NSS changed from year-slash-number system to year plus number in six-digit system.

varied somewhat through the years, the following is one example of the NSS tag used from the mid–1950s to mid–1960s:

"Property of National Screen Service Corporation—licensed for display only in connection with the exhibition of this picture of the theatre. Must be returned immediately thereafter."

The National Screen Service Today: By the 1980s, most of the NSS distribution centers were sold off and eliminated. At this printing, there are only three regional offices remaining in the United States.

When the NSS began to scale down, studios started handling their own printing and distribution. Unfortunately, this change had some negative effects on movie poster collecting. Because each studio was doing its own printing, a lot of the standard sizes were eliminated. These included perennial favorites like half sheets, inserts and window cards. Mini sheets, measuring 11" × 17" to 23" × 35", have taken their places. One sheets, which were always 27" × 41", are still commonly used; however, some studios have opted to print a slightly smaller version, 27" × 40". Apparently, the studios are making these changes in an effort to cut costs.

At its peak, NSS distributed approximately 90 percent of all advertising paper for major studios in the United States. The NSS numbers are occasionally found on movie posters released in today's market.

See also: Benton Card Company; 40" × 60" Posters; Half Sheets; Inserts; Lobby Cards/Sets; Mini Sheets; Movie Art/Paper; One Sheet; Secondary Printers; Six Sheet; 30" × 40" Posters; Twenty Four Sheet; Two Sheet; Three Sheet; Window Cards

Near Mint Condition

What Is Meant by "Near Mint" Condition? A poster or other size movie paper in "Near Mint" condition is one that may have one or two small pin holes in the corner, a few minor wrinkles or small tears in the border only. The artwork is in excellent condition with no blemishes whatsoever.

Depending on the size and type of the movie art, materials in "Near Mint" condition can be folded or rolled, depending on the manner in which they were originally distributed to the theatres and poster exchanges. If the poster/movie paper was initially distributed in a folded condition, as was the case with most large paper sizes that are dated before the 1980s (including one sheets, two sheets, three sheets, six sheets, twenty four sheets), fold lines that are present due to the poster being folded for shipping will not detract from its "Near Mint" condition rating. However, if the poster was folded, or has fold lines not associated with folding it for distribution, then the poster would not be graded as "Near Mint." In addition, smaller card stock materials, such as lobby cards and window cards, were never folded. As such, a lobby card/window card considered in "Near Mint" condition cannot have fold lines. Sizes such as inserts and half sheets were, on occasion, folded by the studio/distributor. If this is the case, then fold lines would not detract from a "Near Mint" rating. However, if the fold lines are the result of some other type of folding, then the item would not be considered in "Near Mint" condition.

Value: A poster in "Near Mint" condition commands slightly less than top dollar for that title's standard retail price range.

Comparison to Nine Category Grading System: The following chart shows

6 Grades	9 Grades	
Mint	Mint	
Near Mint	Near Mint	Some Dealers Classify This Area As Excellent
	Excellent	
Very Good	Very Fine	
	Fine	
Good	Very Good	
	Good	
Fair	Fair	
Poor	Poor	

where a poster in "Near Mint" condition would be placed utilizing the nine category grading system.

See also: Condition

One Sheet

SUMMARY OF FACTS

Size: 27" × 41" (recently 27" × 40") on paper.

History: First introduced and distributed in 1909 by General Film Company.

Purpose: Use in theatre lobbies, theatre marquees, glass displays inside and outside of theatre; balconies and other ad spaces in and around theatres, such as bus, train and subway depots.

Current Usage: Widely used in American and foreign theatre markets.

Notes: More than one version of the one sheet may be released per movie. The different versions are sometimes known referred to as: advance; one sheet style A or B; review; awards, etc.

Prior to 1909, the new movie studios used a variety of means to advertise their films, including painting on crates or displaying black and white pictures. A generic series of posters, similar to those used by vaudeville shows, were commonly used by the early nickelodeons and movie theatres. These posters depicted general scenes of an audience watching a projection or a band playing. Space was left available on these early placards for the theatres to place titles and show times and dates. When the shows changed, the theatre simply slapped new information on top of the old, thus using the same poster over and over again.

In 1909, the main movie studios, which at that time were part of Thomas Edison's Motion Picture Parents Company, formed a movie cartel for the purpose of controlling the production and distribution of all films. This new company was named the General Film Company. Because they controlled most of the movies produced during that time, they were in a position to set industry conformity standards as far as advertising materials were concerned. The first of these advertising tools introduced was the "one sheet" poster.

The one sheet was standardized to a size of 27" × 41". There are a number of stories which relate to the reason why this size was selected. One which seems to prevail throughout the movie art industry is the fact that most printers were unable to produce a sheet 41" long, since most printing presses have a maximum length of 40". By setting the size at 41" in length, only a few printing shops were able to produce the one sheets. In this way, the studios could select and control their printing sources, and make the one sheets harder to copy and reproduce illegally.

The one sheet has evolved over the years due to a number of factors, including advances in printing processes, types of printing paper and the public's changing fancy.

The printing of the one sheets was relegated by the first studios to a select few of lithographers. The first one sheets were printed through a process known as stone lithography. This process involves etching the artwork and print into soft stones, such as limestone, then coating the stones so that the areas etched will retain ink, while the areas of stone without etching are coated to repel ink. This process created a beautiful image of soft colors. After World War I, after many of the stone quarries were destroyed, lithographers substituted limestones with either zinc or aluminum plates. While this process was less expensive, it did not produce the same softness and detail as did the process utilizing limestone.

During the 1930s, offset printing presses were being introduced. This process utilizes planograph printing by indirect image transfer; images transferred from a photomechanical plate or paper mat. Much cheaper and faster, this process soon was utilized by all major movie poster lithographers.

Changing public demand also had a direct effect on the character of movie posters. The appearance of the poster has changed dramatically through the years, depending on what the movie studios perceived the public to want at a particular period of time. The one sheet went from soft detailed colors, to the use of photographs in the artwork, to Art Deco styles. Even the appearance of fan magazines in the 1950s and 1960s affected the way studios designed their one sheets. Today's posters reflect the current climate in America; the fascination with special effects and the draw of graphically detailed subject matter.

Up until the mid–1970s, the paper used to print movie posters was a cheaper grade, a little better than newspaper. In the middle of the 1970s, a new paper was introduced to the printing market. This paper had a clay coating which gave a glossy finish to the poster. Posters on clay coated paper have a smooth feel to the touch, unlike the cheaper paper used for earlier posters which has a coarser feel.

Throughout its history, movie studios would utilize the talents of well-known and recognized commercial artists. However, the artists were not initially allowed to sign their work. In fact, some artists were told to design in a style unlike their own. This continued until the studios recognized that the foreign poster market was utilizing commercial artists and allowing them to sign their names. This then became a norm in the American movie poster market.

The one sheet most commonly measures 27" × 41" and may or may not have a border. It is printed on paper, and is intended to be displayed in a glass "marquee" case. They are rarely used in other locations because they are printed on paper and are not as durable as the other materials printed on heavier paper or cardboard.

One sheets normally include the film's title in large letters at the top, followed by the poster's artwork. The film's credit information is usually found on the bottom of the poster, either within or outside of the artwork. Many posters have a border, and the entirety of the poster fits within that border.

Other information can sometimes be found across the bottom of the one sheet. For example, if the poster was released through the National Screen Service (NSS), their NSS number will be printed at the very bottom along with the NSS tag line (normally beneath the border if there is one). Other indicators may also be on the border such as "Advance," "Teaser," or "Style."

Sometimes a movie studio will issue two or more different one sheets for a particular movie. These are referred to as "styles" and are normally so indicated. One sheets are also released in other forms, such as:

- Advances
- Awards
- Combo Posters
- Rereleases/Reissues
- Review Posters
- Serial Posters
- Special Distribution Posters
- Stock Sheets

Each of these is discussed in detail throughout the Reference section.

Current Usage: The one sheet is still widely used by movie studios in their advertising campaigns. In fact, with the advent of new multi screen theatres, they are sometimes the only movie poster displayed in the theatre lobbies.

There does appear to be a trend, however, to downsize the one sheet to 27" × 40", eliminating the borders. By setting the size at 27" × 40", the artwork can cover the poster from edge to edge. There is also an increase in the number of posters being released with reverse print on the back side. This is known as "double sided" printing. While they are a lot more expensive, they can be displayed in mirror cases, giving a three-dimensional effect. There is a negative to this downsizing, however, in that it has opened up opportunities for more forgeries and reproductions.

Collectibility: Arguably the one sheet is still the most sought-after size and style of movie art among collectors. It is the centerpiece of the movie paper industry and normally commands the highest dollar in relation to other sizes and styles.

While most collectors still pursue the older titles, there is a wave of new collectors who seek newer posters, particularly those posters that are unique in some way. For example, double-sided posters or posters that are printed with holograms or other special effects are extremely desirable among the newer collectors.

See also: Almost all subjects discussed in one way or another relate to the one sheet.

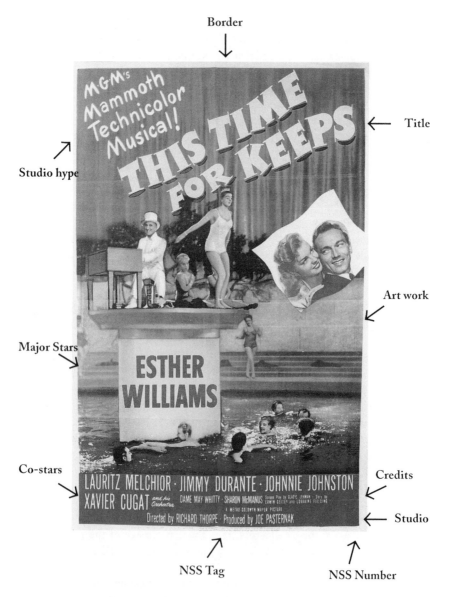

This is considered the standard layout for a one sheet.

Poor Condition

What Is Meant by "Poor" Condition? Posters in "Poor" condition have serious defects such as large tears, large pieces of poster missing, serious fading or in general, and are in such poor shape that even the slightest handling adds to the damage.

Materials in "Poor" condition can be folded or rolled, regardless of the manner in which they were originally distributed to the theatres and poster exchanges.

Value: The value of a poster in "Poor" condition will weigh heavily on its title. If it is a rare piece, it still may command the lower end of the poster's normal price range. A poster in "Poor" condition must be professionally restored.

Comparison to Nine Category Grading System: The following chart shows where a poster in "Poor" condition would be placed utilizing the nine category grading system:

6 Grades	9 Grades	
Mint	Mint	
Near Mint	Near Mint	Some Dealers Classify This Area As Excellent
	Excellent	
Very Good	Very Fine	
	Fine	
Good	Very Good	
	Good	
Fair	Fair	
Poor	Poor	

See also: Condition

Press Books

SUMMARY OF FACTS

Size: Varies.

History: First used in the 1910s as part of campaign kit (now press kit).

Purpose: To provide background on the film and its stars, and any other press-related information.

Current Usage: Widely used.

Notes: Normally included in press kit.

The term "press book" is generic in nature, but has come to mean the flyer, pamphlet, booklet or book that is generally part of a "press kit" or "campaign kit" which contains certain information about a particular film. Press books and related press materials date back to 1910s.

Depending on the film, movie studios release certain data about the film, its stars, crew, or other information that the movie studio deems helpful to a theatre or film exhibitor. Recognizing that many theatre managers did not have an advertising background, the major studios had their advertising departments design and distribute advertising and press materials to the theatres to help in the overall promotion of a film.

Press books come in such a variety of shapes, sizes and forms that there is no way to describe all the possibilities. They can be anywhere from a small one page flyer folded in two to an elaborate 50-page bound book, and anywhere in between. They were also known by a number of different terms, including: "Advertising Manual," "Showman's Manual," and "Merchandising Manual."

Simply put, the press book contained whatever information a studio chose to release on a particular film. Some press books contain background information about the film, the actors, the crew and other information about the film's history. Some contain news articles about the stars' lives outside of the film.

Some press books contain an assortment of the advertising materials that are available to the theatres, such as the various sizes of posters, lobby displays, and banners. Merchandising tie-in products may also be available.

Press books can contain ideas for promotions, radio and television advertising, newspaper and magazine advertising, contests and games.

Current Usage: As part of the press kit, they are extensively used by movie studios.

Collectibility: Because the press books can contain background information on the film and its stars (some information not being available through any other means), they are considered collectible to some collectors. They are also inexpensive, which makes them easier to acquire.

Press books can also be used to help date other movie materials, particularly those prior to the 1940s which were not dated.

See also: Ad Sheets/Slicks; Campaign Kits; Movie Art/Paper, Press Kits

The press book gives the variety of advertising materials available for the theatre to use. This particular movie had a wide variety ranging from a 24 sheet billboard to a herald hand-out.

Press Kits

SUMMARY OF FACTS

Size: Varies.
History: First used in the 1910s.
Purpose: To provide complete materials for press releases, promotions, campaigns for the movie exhibitors.
Current Usage: Widely used.
Notes: Sometimes the term is interchangeable with campaign kit.

The term "press kit" is in actuality a generic term which has come to mean a specific group of materials distributed to movie theatres or film exchanges to help advertise and promote a film. Press kits were distributed by movie studios as early as the 1910s, but were usually referred to at that time as "campaign kits." Although the terms are used interchangeably, most campaign kits were issued for major motion pictures and were therefore more comprehensive than those kits known today as "press kits."

The main purpose of a press kit was to give movie theatres and exhibitors "tools" or "ideas" that could be used for press releases, promotions, contests and advertising suggestions. In other words, a press kit was provided to help the theatre or film distributor with ideas on how to create a successful film campaign.

Because of its inherent generic nature, the form that the press kit took and the items that were a part of it varied from film to film and studio to studio. The movie studios would outline a national campaign based on the potential success of the film and would design their advertising materials accordingly. The early press kits came in all shapes and sizes, too many to even begin to describe. Since the 1980s, many of the film studios have standardized their press kits to some extent, but to this day no two press kits are alike.

Beginning with the 1980s, most major studios adopted a "folder" to hold their press kit materials. If the film is expected to be a hit, the press cover kit will normally contain the name or logo of the film. Most major studios have a standard cover with only the studio's name that they use for all of their minor releases. Some studios will even issue one press kit for a series of movies, for example, a studio's planned summer releases or winter releases. In this case, the press kit cover will normally just contain the studio's name and logo.

Press kits from smaller studios may not even come in a cover. Sometimes the materials are simply placed in an envelope and mailed to the theatres or film distributors.

No two press kits are alike; however, most press kits will contain a few "staple" items. These may include:

- A press book—A book or booklet that normally gives a complete background of the movie, its stars, crew and any interesting information that could be used in press releases.
- Advertising aids—A listing of posters and other advertising and merchandising tie-in products that are available to the theatre or film distributor for use in promoting the film. This is sometimes a part of the press book itself.
- Ad slicks—Advertising blocks in differing sizes that are prepared and ready for submission to newspapers or magazines.
- Black and white stills—Black and white pictures of the stars in certain scenes with full credit information on the bottom. These can be used in a variety of ways for promotional purposes.

If a motion picture is expected to be a huge financial success, sometimes movie studios will release more elaborate press kits. These may contain:

- Buttons—To be distributed to movie patrons or at outside events promoting the movie (such as special screenings).
- Sample posters—Some press kits will come with a one sheet or other size poster for use in the theatre lobby.
- Hats or other merchandising products—Again, to be used as giveaways or special promotions.
- Slides—Slides of scenes from the movie that can be used at special promotions.

In short, press kits are designed by the studios on an individual basis depending on the film. Their final form and content are based solely on the movie studio's overall advertising campaign, and its vision for the film and its potential box-office success.

Current Usage: Because a film's success depends so heavily on its advertising campaign, press kits are as important today as they were in the beginning of the film industry. As such, they are extensively used by most motion picture studios, both large and small. In fact, there are very few films distributed that are not accompanied by some type of press kit, in one form or another, to help the theatres promote the film.

Collectibility: Because some press kits contain so much information about a movie and its cast, and because they contain photographs or other merchandising items that were produced in limits numbers (buttons, hats, etc.), they are very popular with some collectors. In comparison to other sizes of movie art, press kits are usually very inexpensive, and are therefore more affordable and easier to obtain (particularly with older movie classics).

Press kits also offer great insight into the history of a film. Since many of the early posters were not dated, press kits can be used to determine the age of certain movie posters, and are therefore an extremely helpful tool for dating movie materials. This fact also makes them a favorite with some collectors.

See also: Ad Sheets/Slicks; Campaign Kits; Movie Art/Paper; Press Books

Printing Processes/Lithographers

The movie poster first made its appearance at a time when the world was experiencing the industrialization of special printing processes. The poster was used extensively in all forms of advertising, and this was particularly true with the early movie industry.

Over the years, the movie poster went through many changes, some of which were the direct result of evolutions in printing processes. The earliest posters were printed using a process called stone lithography. Posters printed through stone lithography were rich in color and tone. Heavier card stocks posters, just as lobby cards, inserts and window cards, were initially printed using a rotogravure process. In the 1920s, these card stock materials were produced using the photogelatin or heliotype process. Less colorful than stone lithographic versions, posters printed through this process were designed for close viewing only.

By the 1920s, color offset printing was introduced and many of the posters, particularly one sheets and larger sizes, were printed using this new process. For years, studios utilized both the offset printing and stone lithography processes simultaneously. The two posters resulting from these processes can be distinguished by the fact that stone lithographic posters show the grain of the litho crayon while, under magnification, offset posters show the mixing of the dots which are used to create the colors.

The following is a brief look at how these individual processes worked.

Stone Lithography: The term "lithography" actually means printing from flat surfaces. The process, also known as planographic printing, employs the concept that oil and water do not mix.

In 1798, Alois Senefelder of Germany applied this principle to printing. He found that certain porous stones, such as limestone from Alsace, Germany, could absorb both water and oil. By drawing on the stone with a greasy crayon and dampening it with water, the stone would absorb water only where there was no greasy crayon. Senefelder rolled oily printing ink over the stone. The part of stone dampened by the water repelled the ink. By pressing a sheet of paper against the stone, the design made by the ink was transferred to the paper.

This process produced exceptionally rich tone, depth and color. Lithographers would break down the original artwork into separate sections of color components, using a separate stone for each color. After the stones were ingrained, the outline of the artwork for the poster was sketched on the individual stones with non-greasy crayon or ink. Then the drawings were etched into the stone, using equal parts of water and gum acacia mixed with nitric acid. After a cleaning process, the ink and crayon drawings were preserved in stone and resulted in a plate ready for the printing presses.

While producing beautiful posters, these stones were difficult to use and to clean. By the end of World War I, many of the stone quarries were destroyed, and lithographers began using zinc, then aluminum plates in lieu of the stones. When done properly, lithographers could duplicate the rich tones and colors of stone lithography with the zinc and aluminum plates. This process continued to be used to produce one sheets and other larger movie paper until the 1940s, when it was replaced by the more economical color offset process.

Rotogravure Process: Rotogravure process is an *intaglio* method of printing, meaning that the pictures, designs and words are engraved into the printing plate or printing cylinder. Once the copy is photographed, positives are then made from the negatives. The images are transferred to the printing surface by use of carbon tissue covered with light-sensitive gelatin. The gelatin hardens based on the amount of light which passes through the positives. The plate or cylinder is then bathed in acid, which eats through the gelatin squares. On the printing press, the deepest cells retain the most ink and the darkest tones.

The earliest of card stock materials, including lobby cards, inserts and window cards, utilized this process until the 1920s. After this time, most of these materials were being printed using a new process known as photogelatin or collotype printing.

Photogelatin/Collotype: This type of process if similar to lithography. A light-sensitive coating of gelatin is placed on a glass or metal plate. The gelatin is exposed to light under an unscreened negative which carries the image to be printed. The light passes through the negative, hardening the gelatin to varying degrees. The plate is soaked in a solution of water and glycerin.

The hardest areas of the gelatin absorb the least amount of the solution while the softest parts absorb the most. Once on the printing press, the ink adheres to the hardest, driest areas of the plate and prints the darkest tones. The softest, wettest areas take the least amount of ink, creating half tones in subtle gradations to white.

This process was used primarily on card stock materials which were designed to be viewed up close. Because they were not as colorful or detailed, these materials were not as attractive when viewed from a distance. The photogelatin process is similar to that of photo offset, but it shows no dot structure.

Color Offset Printing: Offset printing is a process where the printing is done first on the rubber surface of a rotating cylinder. The impression is transferred to paper by the pressure of other cylinders. The term offset describes the printing, or offsetting, of the ink from the rubber.

Offset lithography is generally accomplished on a press with three cylinders. A lithographic plate of aluminum or zinc is wrapped around the first cylinder. The plate prints on a second cylinder that is covered by a rubber blanket. The impression on the rubber is then printed on the paper which is on the third cylinder. This third cylinder has steel fingers called grippers that hold the paper in position while it is squeezed against the rubber surface.

The use of offset printing for movie posters was first undertaken by Morgan Litho in the 1930s. It was a more economical method, and the offset plates were easier to handle and store. However, although some early examples were able to duplicate the full color of stone litho, posters began to lose their color depth and subtleties as the offset printing process evolved.

Most of the materials printed today by studios are accomplished using this offset printing process, which has been further advanced through the use of computer technology. Today's posters are more defined and detailed, but many collectors do not feel that they can match the lushness of color and tone for which the early stone litho posters were known.

Lithographers: The companies that actually handled the printing of the posters were known as lithographers. For each size of poster in a movie's ad campaign, the movie studio art departments would ship the original artwork to the lithographers. These were known as "reflective" or "hard" art, which meant the original piece of artwork, and a "mechanical" art, which showed the positioning of titles and credit information. Movie companies were very strict about the size and placement of stars' names in relation to the film's title. The lithographers were not allowed to make any changes without checking with the movie studios first.

When the lithographers were through with their posters, they were sent to the individual theatres or poster exchanges, such as National Screen Service exchanges. Larger sizes posters, such as three sheets, six sheets and twenty four sheets were sent directly to the "posting companies" who place them on billboards.

A number of lithography houses lent their expertise and talent to the development and growth of the movie poster in all of its sizes and forms. The Donaldson Print Company printed the American Entertainment Company stock poster of 1900, and alternated with the Miner Litho company for printing jobs for United Artists. Hennegan Show Print in Cincinnati was the lithography house used by Edison for his first programs. They also printed posters for some films released by Triangle Studios. Triangle also utilized the services of United States Printing and Lithograph Company, another New York company, for some of its posters. Edison later contracted with A. B. See Lithograph of Cleveland to handle the Motion Picture Patent Company's printing.

Other lithographers who contributed to movie poster printing included Greenwich Litho who produced posters for Mutual, the distributor of films for Komix, American Film Manufacturing Company, Majestic and Than-houser. Acme Litho of New York handled the advertising for Pathé studios, while another New York lithographer, J. H. Tooker, printed the posters for Vitagraph. Richey Litho Company, Otis Lithographic Company out of Cleveland, Ohio, and H. C. Miner Company were three more New York–based lithography companies. By the 1930s, the big three were considered Joseph H. Tooker Litho Company of New York, Continental Litho Company and Morgan Litho Company.

Lithographer Tag Lines: Many mostly older posters and other materials will carry a tag line which gives the name of the lithographer. Most new materials, however, do not contain the name, but note that it is a "U.S. Litho."

Programs

SUMMARY OF FACTS

Size: Varies.

History: First used in the 1920s.

Purpose: Used as giveaways or sold as souvenirs for special major film presentations.

Current Usage: Rarely used after the 1950s.

Notes: Sometimes sold for ten cents.

Programs were first used in the 1920s, particularly for major motion pictures. Sometimes the studios used them as giveaways to their patrons, while other times they were offered for sale as a souvenir. Their sale price was normally ten cents.

Programs varied in sizes, form and presentation. Most programs, however, consisted of ten to twenty pages chock-full of color spreads, photographs, biographies, advertisements, stories about the stars, information on the film's story line, or any other tidbit that might be of interest to a theatregoer.

Current Usage: Rarely used after the 1950s.

Collectibility: Because programs were designed to be either given or sold to movie patrons, large numbers were produced. As such, they are normally not as hard to acquire and are therefore not very expensive. They are sought after by some collectors, particularly those that like to acquire information about a particular film.

See also: Movie Art/Paper

Souvenir programs could be sold or given away.

Renames

What Are Renames? Renames result when advance movie materials are released under one name, and the movie's title is later changed. The films then can be known under either name, or may carry the notation "a/k/a."

Why Do Renames Occur? Movie titles are subject to change due to a number of circumstances. For example, many films are given working titles and, in some cases, early promotional materials are released with that name. When a subsequent change in the name is made, studios attempt to recover the old material and replace them with new ones.

Sometimes movies that are commercial failures are removed from the market, only to be rereleased years later under a new title. In other solutions, films that certain stars made when they were unknown are later rereleased under a new title to capitalize on their newfound fame.

Another scenario involving renames relates to the titles of American made films that are changed when they are marketed in foreign countries. In any of these cases, the movies can become known by either or both of their titles, and will sometimes carry the notation "a/k/a."

Collectibility: Depending on the circumstances, some renames can become very desirable. This is particularly true when studios release advance advertising materials for popular movies, and then later change the name of the film before it is released. This happened with the second sequel to *Star Wars*. Advance advertising materials were issued to the theatres and theatre exchanges under the title *Revenge of the Jedi*. Although the studio which made the movie attempted to recover all of the materials with the wrong title, a number of them remained on the market. Because there were so few left to collectors, they became extremely sought-after. The popularity of this particular rename was such that a number of fakes also made it to the market.

This Laurel and Hardy movie also includes the original title.

Rereleases/Reissues

What Are Rereleases/Reissues? From time to time, motion pictures are rereleased by the studios to theatres, and when these movies are rereleased, new advertising materials are also reissued and distributed to the theatres. At first glance, some of these reissued materials can look exactly like the original, while others will have noticeable differences.

Distinguishing Rereleases/Reissues from Originals: There are many ways to differentiate original materials from those issued at later times. The following are just some of the more commonly recognizable indicators:

- The use of slogans on the posters such as "Oscar Winner" or "Back by Popular Demand" or similar type slogans which would indicate that the movie has already been released and has won or been nominated for an award.

  Exception: An exception to this would be foreign film festival awards which may precede the release of a film in the United States, such as awards from the Cannes Film Festival.
- The use of the letter "R" in the NSS number located in the bottom right-hand border of the poster. [Note: The initials "NSS" stand for National Screen Service, a nationwide distribution center for movie posters. For more information about NSS, see the entry "National Screen Service."]
- The use of words such as "Reissue" or "Rerelease" somewhere in the body or in the border of the poster.
- The year of the poster's copyright being later than the year the film was originally released to theatres.

Unfortunately, not all materials give an indication that they are rereleases. Some materials will require much further scrutiny. However, there are still a few "not-so-obvious" factors that should be considered. For example:

- Glossy, shiny, slick poster paper was not introduced into the printing industry until the mid–1960s, and was not widely used until the 1970s. Thus, if a poster is for a movie released in 1940 and it is on a slick, glossy paper, chances are that it is a reissue.
- Prior to the 1980s, most movie materials were sent to the theatres in envelopes—thus they had to be folded. Again, if a poster is from a movie released in 1940 and it comes rolled, there is a strong possibility that it is a reissue. It is quite rare to find pre–1980s materials that have not been folded.
- Classic motion pictures such as *The Wizard of Oz* and *Gone with the Wind* are such favorites with the moviegoing public that they are

constantly being rereleased. Finding original materials on any of these films is quite rare—and those materials would be quite expensive. If approached with materials from such classics, one should consult an expert in movie posters from that time period. [Note: Because of their popularity, posters from classic movies are also reproduced commercially when they are released on video and shown on a regular basis on network/cable television; or they may be illegally copied and sold. When making a determination as to a poster's originality, the possibility that the poster may fit into one of these categories must also be considered.

Pre–1940s Materials: There are situations where it is hard to differentiate an original poster from a subsequent reissue. This is particularly true with materials released prior to 1940, and novice collectors should be extremely careful before acquiring anything from this time period. There were several major studios that did not even date their movies released in the 1920s and 1930s. In these cases, more intense scrutiny is necessary, and the best advice would be to talk to a reputable movie poster dealer who is familiar with movie posters from this time period.

Post 1940s Materials: Even posters from more current titles can be confusing when trying to determine an original from a reissue. There are instances where the only difference between an original and a reissued poster is in a small area of the poster which is colored differently. In another case, the "Rating" box is found in a different location on the reissued poster than it was on the original. In these cases, the determination as to whether a poster is an original or a reissue cannot be made on the face of the poster, and more in-depth study is necessary. One option is to contact a reputable movie poster dealer who is knowledgeable about posters from the particular era of the poster. You could choose to do your own research by either contacting the studio or trying to obtain a press kit or press book. Many times, the press book will give you information and photographs which will help you make this determination.

Since the advent of the videocassette market, movie studios rarely rerelease films to the theatres. Instead, once a film makes its theatre run, it is issued on videocassette form for purchase or rental.

Check Before Purchasing: Since there are as many ways to indicate a poster is a reissue as there are posters, this book cannot list all possible scenarios. However, we have listed the most commonly found indicators. Careful scrutiny of a poster should give some indication as to whether it is an original or a reissue. If the poster is a relatively recent, inexpensive one, a careful review of its contents should be adequate to make a reasonably safe purchase. However, if the poster is an older, rare or more expensive piece, in addition to the above clues, other considerations should include: (1) is the seller a reputable dealer

Black Beauty. The National Screen Service number (also called the "NSS" number) which is located in the lower right corner is "R 74/319." The fact that it starts with an "R" indicates that this poster was reissued in 1974. The movie and the original poster were released in 1971.

Enter the Dragon. The National Screen Service number located in the lower right corner is 730268. Since the first numbers in the NSS series indicate the year of the poster's release, it would be assumed that this poster was issued in 1973. However, the copyright information located directly under the words "A Warner Communications Company" indicate that this poster was actually copyrighted and released in 1979.

or a reputable store; (2) does the seller guarantee the originality of the poster; (3) can the materials be returned if they are later determined to be a reissue; and (4) will the seller give you time to do further research. If any of these considerations is not met, it is recommended that you pass on the purchase until you have done further research.

Collectibility: Most movie poster collectors consider the value of reissued materials to be significantly less than that of its original counterpart, and this value continues to decrease with each subsequent reissue. For example, a poster reissued five years after the original release date will be valued less than the original poster, but greater than a poster reissued ten years after the original release date.

Exception 1: One exception to the above involves the materials released for the movie *Asphalt Jungle.* At the time of its release in 1950, Marilyn Monroe had not yet made her impact on Hollywood and was not even mentioned in the film's credits. By 1954, Monroe had become a "superstar," and the producers of *Asphalt Jungle* capitalized on her popularity by rereleasing the movie that year. The one sheet accompanying this rerelease featured a full-length shot of Marilyn Monroe, who was then listed as the star in the credit information. New lobby cards were also reissued featuring Monroe in almost every scene. Because Monroe material is so

Barbarella. The National Screen Service number locate din the lower right hand corner is 770161 indicating that this poster was issued in 1977. Those familiar with the motion picture will know that this movie was originally released in 1968, so ths poster must be a reissue. However, since you cannot be familiar with all movies, a further review of the poster reveals the words "A Paramount Pictures Re-Release" which plainly distinguishes this poster from the original poster.

popular with collectors, the 1954 rereleased materials are considered more valuable than the materials originally released in 1950.

Exception 2: There are so many collectors of *Star Wars* materials that the movie's producers regularly reissue their movie posters and other materials, each time with different graphics and artwork. These materials can generally be distinguished by an "R" at the beginning of the NSS number. There are so many different *Star Wars* posters on the market that a "Poster of Posters" was also released, showing pictures of all of the *Star Wars* posters. While the original *Star Wars* materials are still considered the most valuable of the series, the reissued posters are sought-after collectibles, and the value of these reissued posters is *not* decreased by each subsequent reissue.

See also: Awards; Cable/Network TV Posters; National Screen Service; Video Posters; chapter on Getting Started

Review Posters

What Are Review Posters? Quite often studios will give a special preview of a film to critics before the movie's release to the general public. If there are enough positive comments, they will issue a special style "review" poster with the general release of the film. A review poster *is not a reissue.*

The review poster is normally issued as a one sheet. Because its principal purpose is to bring to light the excellent reviews and special commendations the film has received, the review poster usually lists a number of the positive remarks. To accommodate space for these remarks, the artwork on a review poster is usually very limited. Review posters are normally issued in tandem with regular movie materials.

Spotting a Review Poster: It is very easy to spot a review poster. It has very little or no artwork, little or no credit information, and contains mostly excerpts from newspapers, movie critics, and magazines. Most review posters are simply a listing of favorable comments that were made about the film in the media, with some artwork in the background.

There are some review posters that will have the word "review" printed on the bottom right corner. Not all review posters are so marked, however.

Left: Regular style of *The Great Train Robbery* (which is a British film). *Right:* Same graphics, only smaller, on review poster.

Collectibility: Review posters are a lot less desirable than regular release one sheets, unless a collector is interested in acquiring *all* posters released for a particular film. The review posters are normally unattractive, containing little artwork and plenty of text.

See also: Movie Art/Paper; One Sheet; Styles

Scene Cards

SUMMARY OF FACTS

Size: 8" × 10", 11" × 14"; part of lobby card set.
History: First introduced and distributed in the 1910s.
Purpose: Part of lobby card set.
Current Usage: Lobby cards are issued only in foreign markets.
Notes: Usually includes scenes with major and minor stars.

Scene cards make up the majority of those comprising a lobby card set. Lobby sets were initially introduced in the 1910s.

The term "scene card" can mean any of the cards found in a lobby set that reflect scenes from the movie. These cards normally contain one or more of the film's cast. There are normally six to seven scene cards in a lobby set. A set of lobby cards typically consists of the following:

- Title card usually giving credit information (similar to the one sheet) (1 card)
- Scene cards featuring major stars (2–3 cards)
- Scene cards featuring minor stars (2–3 cards)
- Scenery cards featuring group shots, extras or just scenery. (Also known as the "Dead Card") (1–2 cards)

Many of the lobby card sets are numbered, showing each card's position in the set (that is, 1–8). The title card is always first, and the dead card is usually numbered later in the series, such as no. 8. The scene cards are numbered in the middle. Prior to the 1960s, the lobby card number was usually found in the corner of the artwork on the card. Post 1960s lobby cards normally have numbers that are printed on the bottom border, in typewriter style.

Current Usage: Lobby sets for American-made films are no longer used in American markets. They are, however, used commonly in foreign movie markets.

Collectibility: Following the title card, the lower numbered scene cards are usually the most sought-after because they normally contain scenes with the film's stars. Higher numbered scene cards usually follow in order of preference, with "dead" cards being the least popular with collectors.

See also: Dead Card; Lobby Cards/Sets; Title Cards

Scene Stills

SUMMARY OF FACTS

Size: Usually 8" × 10".

History: First used as early as 1900s.

Purpose: Used for promotional displays and print advertising.

Current Usage: Widely used.

Notes: The first lobby cards issued in 1910s were actually 8" × 10" stills.

The use of 8" × 10" scene stills as a promotional tool dates back to the earliest of films. Long before the appearance of posters, scene stills were used by the earliest nickelodeons as a form of advertising their featured flicks.

Scene stills are standard 8" × 10" glossy photographs, either in black and white or in color. They are normally photos taken of the film's stars on the movie set during the production of the film. Although they are referred to as scene stills, the "scenes" they portray sometimes do not actually make it to the screen.

There is usually some type of descriptive information included on the scene still, such as the title of the movie, the producer or director of the movie, a description of the actual scene and the star or stars that are pictured. Sometimes the studios will type the description on a separate piece of paper and staple it to the scene still.

Current Usage: As part of the press kit, they are extensively used by movie studios.

Collectibility: These scene stills are normally part of a press kit and are therefore collectible as a component part.

See also: Press Kit

Secondary Printers

By the mid–1940s, most major studios had contracted with the National Screen Service (NSS) to handle their national distribution of advertising products. While the posters that were part of the theatre lobby displays were the full color NSS versions, theatres looked for an alternative to the materials that

Copyright 1956, United Artists Corporation. Permission granted for newspaper and magazine reproduction. (Made in U. S. A.)

ROBERT MITCHUM in
Sheldon Reynolds' Full Length Production of
"FOREIGN INTRIGUE"
Introducing GENEVIEVE PAGE and INGRID TULEAN.
Produced, written and directed by Sheldon Reynolds.
In Eastman Color. Released thru United Artists.

"Property of National Screen Service Corp. Licensed for display only in connection with the exhibition of this picture at your theatre. Must be returned immediately thereafter." 56/261

Scene stills have a tag across the bottom of the photo with copyright information (far left). Film title and stars also appears (text in bottom center). Pre–1984 stills of this nature had the NSS tag and NSS number (see bottom right).

were used in greater numbers, such as window cards and heralds. (Window cards were placed in retail and office windows and on utility poles; heralds were handed out directly to the public.) Since the theatres had to purchase these materials in bulk, they looked for a cheaper alternative to the NSS materials.

A number of secondary printers came on the market producing less expensive versions of the window cards and heralds, usually in two or three colors instead of full color. The artwork on these secondary materials can be the same or totally different from the NSS versions.

While there were a number of regional secondary printers that specialized in this type of printing, the materials of the following three printers are most often found in the movie art industry.

Benton Card Company

Of all the secondary printers, Benton Card Company produced the majority of the materials found on the market. Their history and a description of their products can be found under the entry "Benton Card Company."

Globe Poster Printing Corporation

Globe Poster Printing Corporation was formed in 1929 by Norman Goldstein and Mike Shapiro, and they opened their first printing shop in Baltimore. Although they began their business in the middle of the Depression, their business prospered by printing posters for burlesque shows and carnivals. The company extended its business to include posters for entertainers, gospel shows, and even politicians. At one time, Globe printed posters for almost every boxing match in Baltimore, Philadelphia and New York. Globe also produced a limited number of movie posters.

Globe Posters: In 1955 Globe was purchased by Norman Shapiro. He started a new trend in posters by printing over a fluorescent silk screen, giving a "day-glo" appearance. Globe posters from this period are easily recognizable by their flashy and bold colors.

Globe Product Line: In addition to their wide variety of entertainment, sport and political posters, Globe also printed concert tickets, restaurant menus, bumper stickers, T-shirts and ties, from their facilities in Baltimore.

Hatch Show Prints

Hatch Show Print was started in 1879 by brothers C. R. and H. H. Hatch. Their printing business primarily entailed show poster products, such as handbills and posters for vaudeville, minstrel and gospel shows. They later branched into advertising materials for the Grand Ole Opry and the Negro Baseball League. Eventually, Hatch Show Prints began regional distribution of movie materials. The bulk of their movie posters were produced during the 1950s.

Hatch Posters: Hatch Show Print movie posters were printed on a heavy paper stock. The majority of their materials were window card size, although they did produce other sizes. Most of their materials were printed for "B" or low budget movies. Hatch posters were normally printed in one, two or three colors.

The Hatch Show Print materials are distinguishable by their "wood block style." All of their materials were printed on century-old heavy presses, and they utilized hand-carved wood blocks as printing plates. Instead of using separate pieces of wood set by hand, their posters are carved out of one big block of wood.

Hatch Product Line: Hatch Show Print continues to produce advertising materials for today's entertainment market, utilizing the same "wood block" process, from their Nashville facilities.

Collectibility: Many long-time collectors shy away from collecting materials from these "secondary printers." These posters do not command the same dollar value as their NSS counterparts, even though they are the same age, and may be identical to the NSS versions. These materials are finding a market,

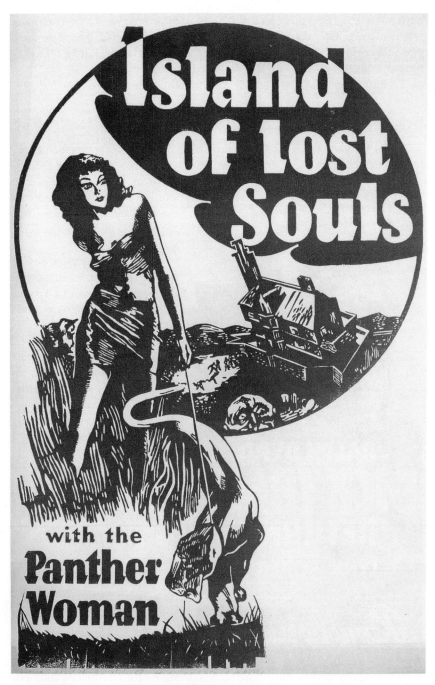

This single color poster has the block style for which Hatch is known.

however, with newer collections for two basic reasons: (1) it is a way to collect original "legitimate" materials at a less expensive price; and (2) because these secondary printers provided the materials for some "B" movies, they are sometimes the only materials available for certain movie titles.

See also: Benton Card Company; National Screen Service

Serial Posters

What Are Serials? A movie serial consists of a series of unfinished chapters or episodes that evolve around one plot, the last chapter bringing the serial to its final conclusion. The words "To Be Continued" are used to end each individual chapter, leading to the final installment.

History of American Serials: Serials were first introduced in the French movie industry in 1908. The first American made serial was *The Adventures of Kathlyn,* which began in December of 1913. The chapters were shown on screen and were simultaneously carried in the *Chicago Tribune.*

The first American sound serial was *Ace of Scotland Yard,* a ten-episode serial released by Universal Studios in 1929. Universal, Columbia, Mascot and Republic, as well as some independents, were the only studios producing serials. The "Big Five"—MGM, Warner Bros., 20th Century–Fox, Paramount and RKO—did not venture into the serial market.

Each serial episode would last about twenty minutes. It would normally be presented after the cartoon shorts and before the feature presentation. The serial chapters would be

The premiere poster usually shows number of chapters in serial. Others would show individual chapters.

shown in sequential order usually on a weekly basis, until reaching its final "spine-tingling" climax.

There were a total of 231 sound serials produced form 1929 until 1956. Batman, Dick Tracy, Buck Rogers, Captain Marvel, Flash Gordon, and The Shadow were just a few of the more popular serial characters. By World War II, the popularity of serials diminished. In 1946, Universal released its final serial, *The Scarlet Horsemen*. Republic continued producing serials until its final release in 1955, *King of the Carnival*. Columbia lasted one more year, and released its last serial, *Blazing the Overland Trail*, in 1956.

Serial Posters: The studios released movie posters for each episode of their serial titles. These posters would have the title of the serial, the artwork and stars, and the chapter number. Some posters even indicate the total number of chapters.

Collectibility: Serial posters have remained a somewhat overlooked area of movie art. By definition, serial posters qualify as "legitimate movie art" because they were issued directly to theatres or film exhibitors for advertising purposes only. However, they are not as sought-after as posters from feature films from the same time periods. There are collectors who do collect serial movie art, and this trend is likely to continue, given the fact that there were only 231 serials produced and the limited number of posters available.

Six Sheet

Summary of Facts

Size: 81" × 81"; printed on paper.
History: First introduced in the 1910s.
Purpose: Used outside in larger advertising spaces; mini billboards.
Current Usage: Rarely used.
Notes: Normally come in 2 to 4 pieces.

Six sheets, along with three sheets, were first introduced during the 1910s, when billboard advertising was gaining popularity and movies moved from one to two reels. The six sheet was designed to be used in larger advertising areas or as small billboards.

Six sheets measure 81" × 81", and got their name from the fact that they are six times the size of one sheet. Movie studios sometimes issued them in two to three different artwork designs.

Because they are mean to be viewed from a distance, the artwork on six sheets is usually coarser looking and lacks the clarity and crispness of the smaller paper. Because of their large size, they normally come in two to four pieces which have to be placed together to make a single display.

Current Usage: Six sheets are rarely used today.

Collectibility: Because of their larger size and the fact that they come in two to four pieces, six sheets are not as widely sought-after as are the smaller sized posters. All parts of the six sheet are necessary to make the poster collectible from a movie art standpoint. Any missing piece renders the poster uncollectible.

There are certain movie art collectors that prefer the larger sized posters. Some collectors like the six sheets because there were fewer of them printed, making less of them available on the market. Because of their size, quite often there are stars pictured on the six sheet that are not on the smaller size posters.

Six sheets are also popular with different types of clubs or theme restaurants, because a six sheet, with all of its parts, can make an entire wall display based on a particular "theme."

See also: Movie Art/Paper

Special Distribution Posters

Special Target Films: Not all films produced are released to "mainstream" theatres. There are many movies made each year that are written and produced with a "special target audience" in mind. Below are some of the types of films that would fall into this category.

- **Documentaries.** Documentaries are generally film presentations that consist of factual, historical, political or social events or circumstances. These films often contain actual news footage and narration. Documentary films normally are released in very limited markets, many times on a regional basis only. War documentaries, particularly those of World War I and World War II, were extremely popular with the moviegoing public.
- **Independent Studio Releases.** Fighting for their slice of the movie pie, many independent film makers have difficulty finding a viewing venue for their films. Since they are "unproven" to the "mainstream" movie industry, these independent films are normally shown only in small, independent theatres and those theatres that are geared toward "art" films.
- **Military Training.** Obviously, the films produced for "military training" are viewed only in military surroundings. These films are not normally found outside the venue of military property.
- **Regional Releases.** Sometimes the subject of a film may be of only regional interest; as such, the film is only released to theatres (usually small independents) within that target region. Regional releases are rarely shown in major theatre chains.

This war documentary shows few of the many stars that served when the war started.

- **Sex Education.** Sex education films are gaining popularity and are shown in schools, churches and social venues. These films are produced strictly for educational purposes and are not designed nor intended as commercial ventures.
- **X-Rated.** Although cable TV has taken a bite out of this market, X-rated movies are still produced and are still shown in X-rated theatres throughout the country. Rarely is an X-rated movie shown in a "mainstream" theatre.

Movie Materials for Special Target Films: Although the budgets for these types of film cannot compete with those of major theatre productions, most of the film producers release advertising materials to go along with their films. Just as these movies are targeted for "special interest" groups, their movie posters are also sought after by "special interest" collectors who prefer collecting the materials on these limited distribution films.

Collectibility: The advertising materials for these types of special target audience films do not share the same widespread acceptance with movie poster collectors as do mainstream movie materials. However, because of their smaller distribution, there are limited numbers available, thus making them harder to obtain.

Many collectors base their poster collections on a particular theme or person. This is also true with "special target audience" film material. There are certain collectors who collect posters and other materials from one or more of these special category films. This is particularly true of X-rated movie materials, independently produced films and those of war documentaries. X-rated posters are often tame in spite of their subject matter. Some well-known actors made their debuts in X-rated films, and many collectors collect these posters for that reason.

Many of the war documentaries produced during World War II were based on the real life heroism of famous people, including some movie stars. The posters from these films are popular with many collectors, particularly those who like the 1940s materials. America's patriotism was at an all-time high during this war, as many of the posters from these documentaries reflect.

While many independently produced films enjoy only limited showings in small theatres, some of these films are so well made that they eventually spill over into the "mainstream" moviegoing arena. This recently occurred with the very popular film *Hoop Dreams.* The posters from these types of "sleepers" can sometimes become very desirable, depending on the popularity of the film.

Posters and materials from regionally released films share the same "limited" exposure as the film itself; therefore, only collectors within that region are normally aware of its existence. Posters from educational and training films also have a market—albeit very limited—as there are certain collectors who collect only posters from these types of films.

X-rated posters were usually more tame than some major film posters. The films are quite often a spoof of major films.

Just as the target audiences for these films are specialized, so is the potential market for the films' advertising materials. There are, however, a limited number of movie poster collectors who are interested only in these types of specialized distribution films. The market for the posters from these films is very limited, and does not compare to the marketability of most "mainstream" materials. However, the fact that these posters are much harder to obtain and are much more specialized makes them desirable to a limited number of collectors.

Special Issues

Special issues is a very broad category representing posters that are printed in a unique way differing from a standard movie poster. Special issues cross over many categories and consequently do not specifically fit into any one category.

Special issue posters are unique and are therefore hard to define. A few examples of a special issue would be as follows:

- **Mylar.** Some special issues are printed on a sheet of mylar plastic, then coated with either silver or gold paint, then the artwork is painted on the silver or gold paint, leaving holes to allow the silver or gold to show through. Mylar posters present a gorgeous image. Because this is an expensive process, usually very few are printed and are more expensive than normal posters.
- **Holograms.** The newest area of special issues involves the use of holograms on movie posters. Hologram posters do not always fall in the limited edition category. For example, the movie poster from the movie *The Santa Clause* incorporated a hologram into the artwork of the film. These were not distributed to the public but were used by the theatres sparingly because of the difficulty in handling this poster. It could not be rolled or folded and had to be shipped flat.
- **Premieres.** For certain major films, studios will hold a special premiere showing at a particular theatre or a few limited theatres. These studios sometimes release a special issue movie poster promoting the premiere. Many times, the movie poster will contain similar artwork to the regular poster, but also include the marquee or some other indicator of the place where the premiere is held. When *Star Wars* premiered, it was shown at four specific theatres, and only two posters for each theatre were made. These are extremely rare and very expensive.

See also: Limited Editions

Stains

A stain results from a number of causes such as water or other liquids spilling on the poster, dirt being rubbed into the poster, and ink or pencil marks being put on the poster. Stains are normally the direct result of accidents, mishandling or abuse. Occasionally, theatre personnel would write messages on the fact of or on the back of the posters.

Effect on Poster's Value: Stains that are present on the border of a poster do not impact the value. However, when the stains deface the artwork of the poster, they are considered serious blemishes and will severely affect the poster's value. Stains that are found on the back of the poster are not considered a defect, unless they result in a bleedthrough or see-through that can be seen on the front of the poster.

Repair/Restoration Options: Water stains and some other liquid or chemical stains can be removed by bleaching/washing the poster. However, this process is extremely delicate and precise because it involves dampening the poster. Because paper is very susceptible to damage when wet, this process *must be done by a professional restorer.*

Light dirt stains can sometimes be removed by a damp cloth, carefully applied to the poster. Posters with stubborn dirt stains should be taken to a professional restorer where different chemicals are available in controlled cleansing processes.

If the stain is the result of an older fountain pen, an ink eradicator can be used to remove the stain. Ink eradicator is a type of bleach, so when the stain is removed, so is the color on the poster. Thus, the area where the ink eradicator is applied would have to be colored in.

If the stain is the result of indelible ink or newer ball-point pens, it cannot be bleached out. *These stains would have to be removed by a professional restorer.*

Pencil stains can be removed with the use of a yellow brick art gum eraser. The art gum eraser is very soft and crumbly. Regular pen and pencil erasers will not only remove the stain, it will also remove all color. *A regular pen or pencil eraser should never be used to remove any type of stains.*

Since removing stains from the artwork of a poster almost always results in the loss of color, *it is highly recommended that the removal of such stains be done by a professional poster restorer only.*

See also: Condition

Standups

SUMMARY OF FACTS

Size: Varies; printing on cardboard.
History: Unknown.

Purpose: Used as large theatre lobby display.
Current Usage: Extensively used.
Notes: Standups vary from countertop to full lobby displays.

Since the term "standup" can mean any type of cardboard display, it is difficult to establish when the first such display was used. It is known that some of the earliest theatres constructed their own "lobby" setups and displays could arguably be considered a "standup." Since "standup" is a generic term, pinpointing a first is virtually impossible.

A standup is considered any type of display that basically "stands on its own" or is able to be displayed with little or no outside support. A standup can range from a small countertop standing display to a larger-than-life lobby-sized display, and anything in between. Most standups are constructed of heavy duty cardboard, since they are designed to stand on their own with little or no outside assistance. Life-sized standups of the stars in a film are very popular lobby displays.

Current Usage: Standups in all forms are extensively used in today's movie theatres. Some of the displays are extremely large, incorporating mobiles, window stickers and other types of advertising materials to complete an elaborate lobby display.

Collectibility: Because many of the standups are "constructed" or put together from a number of pieces to stand, they are sometimes difficult to take apart without any damage. This makes an undamaged used standup rare. Depending on their size, standups are often quite awkward, making them not as desirable as a collectible. However, as with all other forms of movie poster advertising, there are certain collectors who collect standup materials. In addition, a collector may want a particular standup if they happen to like the film.

See also: Movie Art/Paper

Stock Sheets

Stock sheets are posters that are generic in nature, featuring characters in a variety of scenes, not specific to any particular film or title.

When Were Stock Sheets Used? Stock sheets were primarily used for presentations of cartoons or other short films that were provided to theatres along with feature films. These stock sheets could be used over and over as they were not specialized for any particular cartoon or short.

Stock sheets were normally the size of a standard one sheet, 27" × 41". They were generic characters and scenes. Because the art was not specialized to any title, there was no credit information. Stock sheets usually reserved a blank area where a theatre could put a banner giving the name of the cartoon

Stock sheets were common publicity for cartoons and shorts shown before the movie as seen in this 1940 stock sheet.

or short being shown. These banners were designed to be easily removed so that new banners could be used.

Collectibility: Stock sheets are popular with some movie art collectors. This is particular true of stock sheets from the early years and those of popular cartoon characters.

Styles

For major film releases, some studios would issue more than one style of its regular release one sheet or half sheet. Each style was labeled and had its own unique artwork. Because movie companies recognized the diversity of the moviegoing public, they would issue more than one version of their regular release one sheets and half sheets on their big budget films. Attempting to appeal to all segments of the market, each style would reflect artwork directed to a particular group of potential moviegoers. For example, one style may present the film in a romantic light, while the other style would portray the film's action or adventure. This way, the movie studios felt that they were appealing to a larger segment of the public.

While most studios would issue two versions, some would release as many as four different styles at a time. The styles were normally marked as "Style A" or "Style B." These markings were used by the majority of the studios. However, some studios, like MGM, would use "Style C" and "Style D." During the 1930s, some Universal posters were marked as "Style X" and "Style Y." The style notation is normally found on the lower border of the poster.

Most of the time, studios would issue "styles" in their regular release one sheet (27" × 41"). However, some studios would also issue their half sheets in various styles. Again, these were done only for major budget films.

Occasionally, a movie studio would have a preview of an upcoming movie especially for movie critics. Upon getting their comments, if they were favorable, the studio would issue a separate poster at the general release called the review style. This style had less artwork, leaving most of the space for the comments of the critics. Even though this is considered an original issue, it is not considered as desirable as the regular issue.

Collectibility: When movie studios issued several versions of their one sheets or half sheets, they may not have printed the same amount for each style. If that is the case, then the style with the smallest distribution would normally be considered more collectible than the style with the largest distribution. In some cases, one style's artwork may be more desirable. However, in the majority of the cases, the value of the poster will be determined by the title, and not the style of the poster.

See also: Half Sheets; Movie Art/Paper; One Sheets

Subway Sheets
also known as **Two Sheets**

The subway sheet measures 41" × 54". Although it is sometimes referred to as the "two sheet," it is not exactly twice the size of a "one sheet."

Subway sheets are printed on a thicker paper than the one sheets. Most subway sheets contain the same artwork as the advance materials, and are almost always issued as "advances."

Current Usage: Subway sheets still enjoy limited use in New York and surrounding areas. They are rarely used outside of this geographic area.

Collectibility: Some collectors like the subway sheet because there are fewer of them released. They are somewhat large and cumbersome, but because they are printed on a thick paper, they are more durable. Subway sheets are distributed folded.

See also: Movie Art/Paper

Suncoast Movie Company

Suncoast Movie Company is a division of the Musicland Group. They have a chain of retail outlets, normally found in shopping malls, that sell movie merchandising material.

The Suncoast Movie Posters: Suncoast stocks a line of movie posters that are labeled as follows:

This label caused quite a concern among most movie art collectors since legitimate movie art, by its strict definition, is not produced for sale to the public. Legitimate collectibles are created solely for distribution to the theatres.

Some collectors wanted to seek a court order to force Suncoast to remove the label, as it could be misleading, particularly to newer collectors.

A detailed comparison of posters shows the following differences:

1. Suncoast posters are no larger than 40" where their *bordered* theatre counterparts are 41".
2. Suncoast posters are printed on thinner paper than the theatre posters.
3. Posters of any pre–'95 Disney-owned studio had individual numbers on the back—there is *no* number on the Suncoast counterpart.

Because of the obvious differences, we called the regional office of Suncoast to find out more about how they obtain their posters. We were informed that Suncoast receives a special printing of 5,000 posters of each movie title that they stock in their Suncoast retail outlets. These posters are not intended for and are not shipped to theatres.

Collectibility: Based on the definition of "legitimate theatre art," we would have to place these posters in the gray area called "limited editions" because of the limited number available of each. To most hard-line collectors, the Suncoast posters are closer to commercial posters than they are to collectible theatre art.

See also: Commercial Posters; Limited Editions

Tears

Causes: Most tears on posters are found in the area of the fold lines. When posters have been folded and unfolded a number of times, pressure is put on these fold lines, and sometimes this eventually leads to tears. Tears can also be the result of mishandling.

Effect on Poster's Value: The location and size of the tear will determine what effect, if any, it will have on the overall value of the poster. As with other blemishes and defects, if the tears are on the border of the poster, they will not impact the value, generally speaking. If the tear affects the poster's artwork, the overall value of the poster will be decreased.

Repair/Restoration Options: Most tears, particularly those along the fold lines, can be repaired by using non-acid archival tape on the back side of the poster.

See also: Condition

30" × 40" Posters

SUMMARY OF FACTS

Size: 30" × 40"; printed on card stock.
History: First used in the 1930s for certain titles only.
Purpose: Used in theatre lobbies, balconies, and other ad spaces inside and outside theatres, such as bus, train and subway depots.
Current Usage: Very limited current usage.
Notes: Not as commonly used as other paper sizes.

The posters called 30" × 40"s were introduced into the market in the 1930s. They were primarily offered for major motion pictures only. They were used as both inside and outside theatre displays. Their heavy card material made them more durable than paper.

There were several formats used to produce 30" × 40"s. Some were produced on a ten-color silk screen. They were first made available through New York American Display Company, National Screen Accessories.

A very heavy card stock material was used for the printing of 30" × 40"s. Most of them contain the same artwork as the one sheet. The National Screen Service (NSS) number is normally found on the side of the poster, as opposed to the lower bottom as is the case with one sheets. These materials were normally shipped in rolled condition to the theatre exchanges.

Current Usage: This format, 30" × 40", is generally issued only in rare instances.

Collectibility: Because of their larger size, they are not considered as desirable by the majority of collectors. However, there are certain collectors that collect only the larger sized posters, and this size is particularly popular with this group of collectors. Because they normally contained beautiful artwork and were released din smaller numbers, they are sought after by some collectors. Since 30" × 40"s were sent to the exchanges rolled, these materials lose some of their value if they are folded.

See also: Movie Art/Paper

Three Sheet

SUMMARY OF FACTS

Size: 41" × 81"; printed on paper.
History: First introduced in the 1910s.
Purpose: Used for larger advertising spaces.

Title and NSS number are on the sides of both the 30" × 40" and the 40" × 60".

Current Usage: Rarely used.
Notes: Some three sheets come in two parts.

When movies grew from one reel to two, movie studios began introducing other sizes of advertising paper. The three sheet was first used around 1912, and, along with the six sheet, was designed for larger displays.

Three sheets measure 41" × 81", three times the size of the one sheet. They were sometimes issued in more than one artwork design, with one style featuring the same artwork as that of the one sheet. Some three sheets came in two pieces cut horizontally which, when put together, made one display. In these cases, the bottom part of the poster is normally 41" × 54" and the top part is the size of a one sheet (27" × 41").

As with other large sized paper, they are meant to be viewed from a distance. As such, the artwork is usually coarser looking and lacks the clarity and crispness of the smaller paper.

Current Usage: Three sheets are rarely used today.

Collectibility: Because of their larger size and the fact that they can come in two pieces, they are not as popular with most collectors as are the smaller sized posters. If a three sheet was issued in two pieces, both pieces are required to make the poster collectible.

There are certain collectors that only collect the larger sized posters. They like the fact that they were printed in smaller numbers, meaning that fewer are available on the market. Because of their size, quite often there are additional stars pictured on the three sheet that are not on the smaller sized posters.

Three sheets are particularly popular with different types of nightclubs and theme restaurants because they can make an entire wall display based on a particular "theme" with one poster.

See also: Movie Art/Paper

3-D Movie Posters

Posters released promoting 3-D movie presentations (i.e., cinematic displays in three dimensions) are called 3-D movie posters. Special viewing glasses are needed in order to see the movie in its three dimensional form.

Movies in 3-D format were particularly popular in the 1950s. The fact that a movie was 3-D and required special viewing glasses was promoted heavily by the movie studio's marketing departments. As such, most of the posters that were issued for these movies proclaimed the fact that the movie was in 3-D in big bold letters in the body of the poster.

In order to obtain the "three-dimensional" effect, theatres had to utilize special (and expensive) projection equipment. Because of cost considerations, many theatres could not afford the special equipment and would show the movie in the standard format. In order not to mislead the moviegoers, these theatres would simply block out the notation "3-D" and utilize the same movie poster issued by the studios.

Effect on Value: Many times collectors will come across a poster that has a piece of paper or large sticker adhered to the face of the poster. Before assuming that this poster has been repaired, the collector should check to see if there is a "3-D" notation under the paper or sticker. If this is the case, the poster's value is not significantly affected as this is not a defect, but the theatre's "adjustment" to remove the "3-D" notation.

Title Card

SUMMARY OF FACTS

Size: 8" × 10"; 11" × 14".
History: First introduced and distributed in the 1910s.
Purpose: Part of lobby card set.
Current Usage: Lobby cards are issued only in foreign markets.
Notes: The most valuable of all lobby cards.

A title card is the first card in the series that comprises a lobby card set. Lobby sets were initially introduced in the 1910s.

The title card usually has artwork and credit information, and sometimes the same artwork as the one sheets. Most major studios included a title card in their lobby card sets with the exception of Paramount, which did not issue a title card.

A set of lobby cards typically consists of the following:

- *Title card* usually giving credit information (similar to the one sheet) (1 card)
- Scene cards featuring major stars (2–3 cards)
- Scene cards featuring minor stars (2–3 cards)
- Scenery cards featuring a group shot, extras, or just scenery. (Also known as the "Dead Card") (1–2 cards)

Many of the lobby card sets are numbered, showing each card's position in the set (that is, 1–8). The title card is always first, and the dead card is usually numbered later in the series, such as no. 8. The scene cards are numbered in the middle. Prior to the 1960s, the lobby card number was usually found in the corner of the artwork on the card. Post 1960s lobby cards normally have numbers that are printed on the bottom border, in typewriter style.

Current Usage: Lobby sets for American-made films are no longer used in American markets. They are, however, used commonly in foreign movie markets.

Collectibility: The title card or the first card in the series of lobby cards is considered by most collectors to be the most desirable, particularly because it usually contains the movie's credit information. Title cards are fast becoming one of the more popular forms of movie art collecting.

See also: Dead Card; Movie Art/Paper; Scene Cards; Title Cards

Trimming

Trimming is always an intentional act which is normally done to either reduce the poster to a smaller size, particularly for framing purposes; to intentionally remove the credit information from the poster's artwork; or to remove some type of border defect.

Effect on Poster's Value: Except in the rarest of cases, posters should never be trimmed, as this is considered a serious defect and significantly affects the value of the poster. Trimming commonly occurs on window cards, where blank borders which were designed for use by theatres to put show dates and times are cut off. This diminishes the value of the window card.

Repair/Restoration Options: Professional poster restorers can restore a trimmed poster through a linen backing process.

See also: Condition

Twelve Sheet

SUMMARY OF FACTS

Size: 9' × 12'; small billboard paper.
History: Used in 1940s.
Purpose: Used as small billboard advertising.
Current Usage: No longer used.
Notes: Used primarily by Paramount.

The twelve sheet enjoyed limited use by Paramount Studios in the 1940s. It was used for small billboard advertising.

The twelve sheet, which measured 9' × 12', was introduced by Paramount Studios, and was used almost exclusively by them for a small period of time during the 1940s.

It was intended to be used as a smaller alternative to the twenty four sheet. It proved to be an unpopular size and was discontinued.

Current Usage: No longer used.

Collectibility: Since Paramount was virtually the only studio utilizing this size, and because only a small number were initially printed, twelve sheets are extremely rare. Most of them were destroyed when they were being removed from the billboard.

Twenty Four Sheet

SUMMARY OF FACTS

Size: 246" × 108"; billboard paper.
History: First introduced in 1915.
Purpose: Used as large billboard advertising.
Current Usage: Rarely used.
Notes: Extremely popular in the 1920s.

Billboard advertising was first introduced around World War I and steadily gained popularity. Movie studios first introduced the use of the twenty four sheet for movie advertising in 1915, at the same time that movies grew from two to five reels.

The twenty four sheet measured 246" × 108", and was used primarily for billboard advertising, although some were placed on the sides of large buildings. Their artwork was designed to catch the attention of motorists as they drove by.

Because of the cost involved in printing such a large poster, twenty four sheets were only issued for major motion pictures.

Current Usage: Twenty four sheets are rarely used today.

Collectibility: Very few twenty four sheets are available in the movie art market. They were printed in limited numbers because they were used rather sparingly by movie studios. Unfortunately, most of them were destroyed when they were being removed from the billboard. Therefore, a twenty four sheet that is intact would be quite hard to find. There are very few collectors who handle this size because it is so large. Because of their size, quite often there are additional stars pictured on the twenty four sheet that are not on the smaller size posters.

Twenty four sheets are particularly popular with theme clubs, as one poster can cover an entire wall.

See also: Movie Art/Paper

Very Good Condition

What Is Meant by "Very Good" Condition? A poster or other size movie paper in "Very Good" condition is one that can have multiple holes or small tears in the border, each measuring up to one inch. There can be some minor fading, or small tears in the artwork along the fold lines only. The poster can also have writing, marks, tape, or stains in the border area.

Materials in "Very Good" condition can be folded or rolled, regardless of

6 Grades	9 Grades	
Mint	Mint	
Near Mint	Near Mint	Some Dealers Classify This Area As Excellent
	Excellent	
Very Good	Very Fine	
	Fine	
Good	Very Good	
	Good	
Fair	Fair	
Poor	Poor	

the manner in which they were originally distributed to the theatres and poster exchanges, as long as the fold lines are neat.

Value: A poster in "Very Good" condition commands slightly less than one in "Near Mint" condition for that title's standard retail price range.

Comparison to the Nine Category Grading System: The following chart shows where a poster in "Very Good" condition would be placed utilizing the nine category grading system.

See also: Condition

Video Posters

Video posters are a major part of the paper advertising materials that movie studios provide *to videocassette dealers and outlets for advertising the movie's videocassette for rental or purchase.*

At the beginning of the industry, most of the movies put on videocassettes were those that made a theatrical run and then were later released on video. The movie studios did not issue movie materials specifically designed for the video industry. Instead, they would take the theatre movie posters and place a tag somewhere on the poster to indicate that it was for videocassette purposes. As cable TV began to compete with the video market, and as independent film makers (without the distribution budgets to get to theatres) found a welcome market in video stores, a deluge of movies began to hit the video stores that never made a theatre run.

As more and more consumers purchased videocassette players, the movie studios began to see the revenue potential in the video market. In order to compete with the independents, these studios began to create and issue advertising materials specifically designed for the video market. More and more video posters carried entirely different artwork than theatre posters.

Video direct movies that bypass the theatres are gaining in popularity, particularly in the areas of science fiction and action. Studios like Full Moon and Vidmark release posters with great artwork to coincide with the release of their movies directly to videocassettes.

Distinguishing Video from Theatre Posters: In some cases, a movie studio will issue video posters that have the same artwork as that of the theatre poster. There are several ways to distinguish a video poster from a theatre poster. Here are a few:

- The video poster will have a tag along the bottom or in the middle (sometimes within the credit information) which says something like "Available on Videocassette."
- Most studio-produced video posters will have a notation of "Home Video" on their logo.
- Video posters are never printed in reverse double-sided printing. There are double-sided video posters; however, each side will portray a different movie.
- Many video posters will contain a price sticker or an indication of another movie available for sale.
- Video posters come in a great variety of sizes, including as small as 23" × 35" and up.

Collectibility: Video posters represent another of the "gray areas" in movie art collecting. By definition, they are not "legitimate theatre art" as they were not intended for or sent directly to theatres or film exchanges. In the beginning, movie studios merely plastered a video sticker across a theatre sheet and called it a video poster. Movie art collectors merely thumbed their nose at this "trash" paper. However, when the number of video direct movies increased, some movie art collectors experienced a change in point of view.

For example, many collectors base their collections on a particular star. If that star happens to be in a movie that is released directly to video (bypassing the theatre), there will be no "legitimate theatre" counterpart. In order to maintain a comprehensive collection, many collectors find themselves adding video posters.

Another fact that is lending credibility to video posters is the fact that some movie studios are releasing totally different artwork on their video posters. In some cases, the video poster's artwork is actually more attractive than the theatre poster. Certain collectors like to collect "everything" produced on a certain film. In this case, the video poster would be desirable.

Some of the posters for video direct movies are exceptionally well done, thus making them desirable to some collectors.

Left: Advance poster was sent to the theatres and then the studio changed and released the movie to video instead. *Right:* Theatre poster for *Poltergeist.* Studio put a sticker on it and sent it to the video stores.

For conservative movie art collectors, video posters do not meet the strict criteria of "theatre art" and are still not acceptable as movie art. But for the more liberal or specialized collectors, video posters are being viewed in a more positive light.

Window Cards

SUMMARY OF FACTS

Size: Standard—14" × 22" (untrimmed); Midget—8" × 14" (untrimmed); Jumbo—22" × 28" (vertical); on card stock.

History: First used in the 1910s.

Purpose: For display in businesses' windows around local theatres and throughout the community.

Current Usage: Phased out during the 1970s.

Notes: Printed in larger numbers than other forms of movie art because they were meant to be displayed in areas outside of theatres.

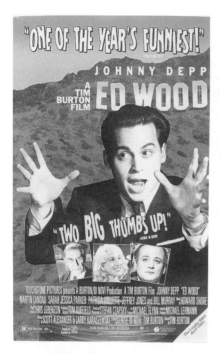 

Left: **Totally different artwork on video version of** *Ed Wood.* *Right:* **Theatre release of** *Ed Wood.*

Standard sized window cards (14" × 22") were first introduced in the 1910s, shortly after the one sheet and lobby cards. The earliest window cards were produced in both the standard and the jumbo (22" × 28") sizes. Midget window cards (8" × 14") were not introduced until the 1930s.

Window cards were initially printed by the movie studios and the National Screen Service (NSS) on cheap card stock, which made them more versatile than the paper materials. They were printed in large numbers so that they could be placed in windows of stores, doctor and dental offices, bakers and on telephone poles in and around a community.

Window cards were initially printed using a brown-and-white roto-gravure process (an intaglio printing process using letters and pictures which are transferred from an etched copper cylinder to paper). In the 1920s, studios began producing their card stock materials through a process known as pho-togelatin/collotype (a printing process utilizing a plate with a gelatin surface carrying the image to be reproduced) or heliotype (a printing process utilizing a photomechanically produced plate for pictures or type made by exposing a gelatin film under a negative, hardening it with chrome aluminum and printing directly from it). This process initially offered one, later two, then three colors.

Because this process utilized duller dyes than did lithography (a printing process whereby an image is imprinted on a limestone, sheet zinc or aluminum and treated so that it will retain ink, while the non-image area is treated to repel ink—this process was utilized for one sheets and larger paper), the colors of the window cards look better close up than they do when viewed from a distance.

In the 1940s, several independent printing houses began releasing less expensive versions of the NSS-produced window cards. These cheaper alternatives were particularly popular with small city theatres and theatres located in rural areas. Because window cards were purchased in bulk, the independently-produced window cards were much more cost effective for the theatres and film exchanges.

The three main independent printing houses known for their window cards were Benton Card Company, Globe Company and Hatch Show Prints. Studio/NSS–produced window cards come in three sizes:

- Standard—measuring 14" × 22"
- Midget—measuring 8" × 14"
- Jumbo—measuring 22" × 28" with vertical orientation

Window cards were printed on a heavier, cheaper card stock material. Because they were meant to be displayed in businesses throughout an area, theatres would normally purchase them in bulk. To keep the costs down, the window cards were printed using a cheaper process; thus, window cards lack the color, detail and splendor of other sizes of movie posters. This is particularly true of the window cards produced by the independent printers.

- **Studio/NSS–Produced Window Cards.** The artwork on the window cards released by movie studios or the NSS may or may not be the same as that of the one sheet. They are normally printed in full color, but lack the detail, color and artwork found on other sized posters. The standard window cards have a top blank border of approximately four to six inches. This border was used by the theatre to write in the dates and show times of the featured film. Sometimes the theatres would staple paper banners with the theatre's name in this blank area. Midget window cards also have a border on the top. Jumbo window cards do not.
- **Independently Produced Window Cards.** The independent printers began producing their version of the standard sized window cards around the 1940s. Because their main intent was to provide an even cheaper window card for use by theatres and film exchanges, the window cards produced by these independent printers were even more

lackluster than the movie studio versions. Most of the window cards were printed in either one, two or three colors (monotone, duotone, tritone). The artwork was normally different from the studio/NSS–produced materials.

Current Usage: Window cards were designed as a "mass advertising" tool, for display in windows in and around a community. However, around the 1970s, advertising strategies changed and window cards in all three sizes were phased out. Movie studios felt they could better utilize advertising dollars in television, radio and newspaper advertising.

Collectibility: Because window cards were produced in large quantities, they are not considered as valuable as other sizes of posters. Within the category of window cards, there is a wide disparity in the value of studio-produced window cards and those produced by independent printers. Studio/NSS–produced window cards are considerably more collectible than those that were independently produced. In fact, some collectors do not even consider the independently-produced window cards to have any value at all.

Window cards, particularly those produced by the studios or the NSS, are popular with some collectors because of their frameable size and because they are cheaper to obtain than other materials from the same time period. Even independently-produced window cards are considered collectible to some, as this may represent the only opportunity to acquire materials on a particular movie.

Window cards were normally shipped to the theatre or film exhibitors flat. Since they were normally not originally folded, window cards lose their value if they contain fold lines or creases. Window cards also lose their value if the top blank border has been trimmed off. Writing or other printing on the blank border of a window card does not affect its value as a collectible.

See also: Benton Card Company; Jumbo Window Cards; Midget Window Cards; Movie Art/Paper; National Screen Service; Secondary Printers

Wrinkles

Wrinkles are lines that are created by pressing, folding or crinkling paper or card stock materials. They are usually not as embedded as creases. Some collectors misclassify wrinkles as creases; wrinkles are not as deep or as damaging as creases. Creases go deeper into the paper and can actually take away the color leaving a white space. Wrinkles are considered surface defects and normally do not take away the color or leave white marks. This is particularly obvious with post–1970s materials which are clay-coated. Creases will actually break through the clay coating and into the color, whereas wrinkles do not.

Causes: Wrinkles are most commonly the result of mishandling, such as rolling posters with rubber bands, laying things on top of them, grasping them too tightly, and bumping the edges.

Effect on Poster's Value: Wrinkles have a minor effect on a poster's overall value, depending on how many there are. This is due to the fact that most wrinkles can be easily steamed out. Wrinkles in the border would have little or no effect; wrinkles on the artwork would have limited impact, depending on the number and severity.

Repair/Restoration Options: Most wrinkles can be removed by either utilizing a heavy duty clothes steamer or a heat press. Even though it is a simple process, care should be taken any time one is handling a poster. If there are any doubts or if the poster is valuable in some respect, a professional restorer should be contacted.

See also: Condition

Foreign Posters

The Foreign Movie Market

Foreign movie material is so vast that volumes could be written on each country. Nothing is standard—oddities and exceptions are frequent—so there is no way, by any stretch of the imagination, to cover this topic. Consider for a moment that this reference manual is dedicated almost entirely to American posters. The same aspects could be written about movie materials for each country. As such, this chapter will try to touch on the more common types of foreign movie materials that are found in the U.S. movie art market.

People in the United States seem to believe that American movies were the first, and that they dominate the world market. That is because so few foreign films are shown here. However, it may be surprising to find out a few truths about movies. For example:

- The first movies were made in France.
- The first movie posters were issued in France.
- The first feature film (over one hour in length) was made in Australia in 1906. Feature films followed in France (1909), Denmark (1911), Germany (1911), Italy (1911), Poland (1911), Russia (1911), Serbia (1911), Spain (1911), Austria (1912), Greece (1912), Hungary (1912), Japan (1912), Norway (1912), Romania (1912), United Kingdom (1912) and then finally the United States in 1912.
- The first 3-D cartoon was released in Canada.
- The first feature length cartoon film was *El Apostol*, released in Argentina in 1917. The first full length cartoon talkie was *Peludopolis*, also from Argentina, released in 1931. *The Adventures of Pinocchio* was released in Italy in 1936. All three of these films preceded the first U.S. cartoon feature, Walt Disney's *Snow White and the Seven Dwarfs*, which was released in 1937. *Snow White* was, however, the world's first cartoon feature to be made in both sound and color.
- The world output of full length feature films is around 4,000 films annually. Almost one-half of these films are produced in Asia, the

largest producer being India, who releases over 700 movies per year. This compares to the approximately 300 films released in the United States annually.

- Many American movie stars, who had difficulty finding steady work in the United States, went abroad and launched their careers. Two of these stars are Josephine Baker and Clint Eastwood.
- Many well-known U.S. stars would make cameo appearances in foreign movies just to tide them over through slow times in U.S. movies.
- Many stars who we consider American are actually foreign actors who started their careers in their native country and then became successful stars in the United States. These include stars such as Christopher Lee, Mel Gibson, Michael J. Fox, and Arnold Schwarzenegger.

In reality, American movies represent a small portion of the world's movie industry. Consequently, American movie posters represent a proportional piece of the worldwide movie art industry, and foreign posters represent a whole other world.

Foreign poster hunting can be exciting and rewarding, but can also be extremely confusing. The foreign poster market is too vast to have any one expert knowledgeable in all areas. In fact, experts quite often disagree among themselves on certain aspects relating to foreign posters.

Taking all of this into consideration, this chapter addresses foreign posters in a very broad and general sense—trying to concentrate on the major countries and assisting beginners and intermediates with some of the basics of various country's foreign poster market.

What Qualifies as a Foreign Poster

The term "foreign" is extremely generic in nature and actually encompasses these specific types of movies:

1. American movies that are released in foreign countries (for example, an American movie released in France);
2. A foreign country's own films released in their country (for example, a Japanese movie released in Japan);
3. One foreign country's films that are released into another foreign market (for example, an Italian movie released in France).

Collectibility

Foreign posters are very popular with some collectors. Some like to collect foreign posters from a particular country. Many collectors try to acquire all the posters from a particular movie, particularly the foreign versions of U.S. films. Still other collectors like foreign movies because a foreign version of an American classic is normally much less expensive. Many collectors like the foreign posters because the artwork is different. In fact, in many countries, poster artwork is much less restrictive and much more risqué, making them more desirable to certain collectors.

When considering collecting foreign posters, a collector may want to concentrate on a particular category of foreign posters or may wish to collect posters from foreign movies that contain American stars.

A Look at Posters from Individual Countries

The following is a brief look at some of the more common foreign posters found in the movie art industry.

Australia

Australia produces 25–60 films per year. Because the country is English-speaking, many of their movies are shown in the United States. Some of Australia's box office hits include *Mad Max* (enter Mel Gibson) and *Crocodile Dundee* (enter Paul Hogan).

The Australian one sheet is the same size as the U.S. version, 27"×41". However, their most popular size is the 13"×30" daybills.

The Australian daybills printed for American-made movies are gaining popularity with some

Australian daybills of American movies are becoming very popular with American collectors. (From the collection of Tony Calvert.)

American collectors. This is because they most often have different artwork, but the text is still printed in English.

Most of the older Australian posters have the name of the printer tagged on the bottom border. The newer Australian daybills do not have the printer's name on the bottom.

ROBERT BURTON PTY. LTD. SYDNEY

Belgium

Belgian movie posters of American-made movies are becoming more popular with some collectors because they usually have different artwork than the American versions. The Belgian posters of American movies normally have the English title printed in parentheses under the movie's Belgian title.

The title in English and two other languages. Notice the Belgian stamp on the lower right.

The most common sizes of Belgian posters are 14" in width and range from 19" to 22" in length. The next most common size is approximately 24"×33".

Many of the Belgian posters have a stamp, somewhere on either the front or back of the poster. Sometimes Belgian posters will have titles written in two or more languages.

Canada

Canada has a very prominent movie making operation. Because the majority of the Canadian population is English-speaking and shares an open border with the United States, a lot of Canadian materials are mixed in without much notice.

United States materials

sent to Canada and then brought back to the United States will sometimes have a stamp (if older) or a sticker (if newer) as follows:

Canada also has a large French-speaking population, so many of their movie posters are printed in French. For the French posters, there are three areas to be considered:

• American movie posters that are printed in French usually do not have a Canadian sticker.

• French movie posters released in Canada usually do not have the Canadian sticker.

• Foreign movie posters that are brought into Canada quite often have the Canadian stickers attached.

These stickers are normally applied with a type of glue that allows easy removal of the Canadian sticker.

Most of the posters (those printed in English or French) released in Canada are one sheet size. There are smaller French posters that are brought into Canada. These are discussed in the next section.

France

France produces about 160 films per year. French movie posters normally come in three dominant sizes. The small French poster measures approximately 15"×22" (this size varies slightly). Their medium size poster is approximately the size of an American one sheet. The large poster measures 47"×63" and is issued in one sheet.

Left: Bland photography for *Mr. Mom*. *Right:* Totally different artwork. Notice the Canadian sticker on bottom.

Sequel movie *Hulk 2* in France but in the United States it was chopped and released as a television series.

Posters of American-made films are printed in the French language. They usually have the title in French (and quite often they change the title so it is not just a French translation of the American title) with the American title listed in parentheses underneath. Quite often the artwork is totally different from the American poster. For collectors who collect certain movie stars, this is fantastic. The French posters normally contain beautiful artwork.

There are quite a few American stars that have made French movies that were never released in America. There are also some American television shows that are released in France as feature movies.

The French movie makers are known for coproducing films with other coun-

tries. Therefore, many foreign posters are actually
Italian/French movies, Afri-
can/French movies, Ger-
man/French movies, and so
on. This makes things
extremely difficult to catego-
rize.

The French also import
a lot of foreign movies
besides American. It is very
common to see a Japanese
film printed in French.

Great Britain

Of all foreign cate-
gories, this is probably the
most confusing to new collectors. There are three basic
classes of British posters.

- British-made films
- British quads
- British (American movies)

These are not to be
confused with International posters (see page 160).

The French are less restrictive on their artwork, so
French posters are often racier than American
posters. For example, collectors of skiing material
could never find this example in the American
movie market.

BRITISH-MADE FILMS

The American movie industry and the British movie industry are so
closely knit that most of the American studios have sister studios in Great
Britain. Quite often, parts of the movies are made in both countries and put
together. There are some major productions that are considered by most to be
American and are actually British (examples are *Bridge on the River Kwai,
Lawrence of Arabia, 2001: A Space Odyssey* and James Bond movies).

The problem is that most British-produced movie posters are not marked
differently from American movie posters. The only way to determine the country of origin is to check the press book to see where the production was made.
This cannot be determined by just looking at the poster.

The British Quad

The next category of British poster is known as the "British Quad." It is released in horizontal fashion, like a larger version of a half sheet. The British use totally different artwork than the one sheets. The normal size of a quad is 30"×40".

Because of the different artwork, British quads are usually very popular with collectors because the artwork on the quad is not found on any American poster. [Note: Quite often the British Quads are brought over to the United States and reproductions are made on cheaper paper. The reproductions are usually quite easy to spot because they are a smaller size, averaging 27"×39" or a close variation.]

Different artwork in a horizontal style makes British Quads very popular with American collectors.

British (American) Posters

The "British" poster is actually a poster of a popular American film, such as *Star Wars, Blade Runner, Lost Boys,* or *Star Trek* that is printed in Europe and sent back to the American market. These posters are normally rolled and printed on a glossier paper than the original American one sheet. These factors normally make them much prettier than the original poster. It is normally one inch shorter than the one sheet size.

Even though new collectors are accepting them, older conservative collectors consider them a nightmare. Unlike the traditional movie poster, when more of these posters are in demand, more are printed, making them closer to commercial posters than to "legitimate theatre art." These posters do not increase in value like the American originals.

Italy

Italy has a very active movie production industry. Besides releasing about 130 films per year, Italy is very active in joint venture movie productions with other countries. Quite frequently, you can find a French/Italian movie or a German/Italian movie.

Italians have been a major force on the American market, producing the spaghetti westerns—the movies that catapulted Clint Eastwood and others into stardom. The Italian movie producers are also responsible for a series of cult favorites, such as *Dracula, Goliath, Hercules & Samson.* What movie buff could forget such classics as *Orgy of the Vampires* or *When Women Lost Their Tails?*

American movie posters printed in Italian will list a studio name, with (ROME) beside it, somewhere in the credit information. As far as Italian movie posters are concerned, most will contain the word "ROMA" somewhere in the border or at the bottom of the credits. There are very few exceptions to this. The most common Italian poster sizes are 13"×27½", 39"×55" and 55"×78".

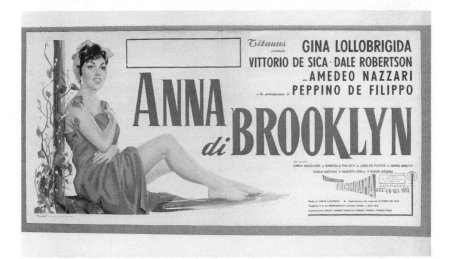

Poster printed horizontally instead of vertically. Notice seal and stamp on the right. (From the collection of Tony Calvert.)

Great Italian poster of Disney shorts. Notice the stamp on top. (From the collection of Tony Calvert.)

International

The term "international" has been used for two different and distinct categories.

One group represents American movie posters that are made to be used in any English-speaking country. These posters are 27"×41" and contain no National Screen Service (NSS) number of tag. The poster will usually have the title and the world "International" printed in the border. (See clip below.)

Beware: There are quite a few reproductions on the market, particularly of older, more sought-after titles.

The second category is a group of very cheaply made reproductions that are produced for major films. The normal size is approximately 26"×38" and these are available on movie classics, such as Marilyn Monroe films, Elvis Presley films, *Gone with the Wind*, and *Casablanca*. This category of international posters is sold at ridiculously low prices for classics. These are no better than cheap commercial prints marketed under the guise of being international posters.

"THE GOOD THE BAD AND THE UGLY" INT'L 1 SHEET

Japan

The Japanese are great film enthusiasts, producing about 250 films per year. Even though we see relatively few here in the United States, the Japanese have had an influence on the American movie industry. Who has not been affected by Kung Fu Theatre or marveled at how many times Tokyo can be flattened by Godzilla and his unending gang of monsters? The comic and animation world has been greatly enhanced by "Japanimation" and rocked over by the Mighty Morphin Power Rangers.

As far as American movies are concerned, the Japanese love to take American movie poster artwork and create collages or rearrange the appearance of the art. The normal sizes of Japanese posters range greatly from 20" to 24" in width and 28" to 34" in length. It is rare to find a year printed on a Japanese poster. This makes them very hard to date. Quite often, the movie's stars are not listed, making cross-referencing extremely difficult.

Art work rearranged for the Japanese version of *Star Wars.*

Mexico

Mexico produces approximately 50 to 100 films per year. They also enjoy a very active movie poster industry. Numerous American stars have crossed the border to make Mexican movies between American film projects.

Older Mexican posters are extremely cheap, newspaper grade paper. This makes them extremely delicate and difficult to handle. These posters are normally 26"×39". They utilized a lot of brown tones and contain some beautiful artwork.

In the mid–1970s, once clay-coating became popular, Mexican posters took on a more "American" look, measuring 27"×41" with a gloss coating.

Almost all Mexico posters contain the tag "Printed in Mexico" on the bottom border.

The Mexican lobby cards, which measure 14"×17" are larger and sometimes more colorful than the American lobby card, and are quite popular with American collectors. If a Mexican lobby card for an American movie has a Mexican distributing company listed instead of the studio emblem, it is most likely a reissue.

Lon Chaney played Wolfman and Frankenstein in *La Casa del Terror* and somehow never spoke a word.

Unusual artwork is making Mexican lobby cards of growing interest to collectors. (From collection of Tony Calvert.)

Poland

Polish movie posters have some of the most beautiful and creative artwork in the movie art industry, particularly those that were produced before 1980. The majority of the posters are done in a style which indicates that they did not have the studio's artwork at their disposal, leaving the artists to use their own imaginations. Many of the posters have a very "artsy" look. Most of the Polish posters are signed.

The Polish posters range greatly in size. The small sizes average 16" to 20" in width and 30" to 33" in length. The larger sizes are normally 26"×39" or 27"×41".

Unfortunately, a cheaper paper was normally used, making Polish posters more delicate to handle.

Polish artwork is some of the most creative and usually contains the signature of the artist.

Getting Started

You now find yourself standing at the threshold—your love of movies and "collector's spirit" compels you to step into the world of movie art—now what?

It is very easy to become a movie art collector. Becoming a "knowledgeable" one takes longer. However, if you follow these simple guidelines, collecting movie art can be fun and rewarding:

- Learn about the movie art industry
- Familiarize yourself with the current movie art market
- Develop reputable sources for your materials
- Learn the proper way to handle and store your posters
- Don't get taken

Before beginning, you may want to give a little consideration to the following. If you are currently a collector, chances are that you have already decided on the type of movie art you want to collect. If you are not already a movie art collector, or are just beginning to collect, you may want to limit your collection to a specific category or grouping. There are so many directions that a movie art collection can take given the number of movies that have been and will be produced. By narrowing your collection to meet certain criteria, you can: (1) become more knowledgeable about a specific area of the movie art market; (2) develop reputable sources for obtaining these specific materials; (3) meet others who share in your particular area of interest for conversations and trades; and (4) make more cost-effective purchases.

While some collectors have no general guidelines which they follow when purchasing movie art and will purchase anything that is pleasing and affordable to them, many collectors choose to narrow their collections to meet certain criteria. Here are a few examples of collecting criteria:

- **By size.** Collecting only a particular size of movie art, such as one sheets, lobby cards or window cards.
- **By era.** Collecting only posters from a particular era or decade, such as '30s, '50s, '70s or '90s.

165

- **By genre.** Collecting only posters from a particular class of films, such as animation, horror, science fiction, musicals or westerns.
- **By title.** Collecting every size, style and type of poster available for a particular movie, including all subsequent reissues, special editions and foreign versions (for example, *Star Wars, Star Trek*).
- **By star.** Collecting posters from films of a particular movie star, such as John Wayne or Keanu Reeves.
- **By studio.** Collecting posters from films produced by a certain studio, such as Universal or Republic.
- **By director/producer.** Collecting posters from movies based on their director or producer, such as Francis Ford Coppola, Steven Spielberg or Alfred Hitchcock.
- **By artists/signed art.** Collecting only those posters signed by either a particular artist or those that are signed by any artist, such as Drew, Bakshi or Peak.
- **By subject.** Collecting posters based on the subject matter of the film, such as diving, automobile racing, or teen exploitation.
- **Foreign films.** Collecting posters from foreign films or collecting foreign versions of posters from American films.

In some cases, particular categories or types of posters just naturally attract certain collectors, and this attraction is the reason why many collectors begin. However, if there is no "immediate draw" to a particular type or genre, new collectors may want to give a little thought to a possible direction before beginning their collections.

Learn About the Movie Art Industry

The first step to becoming a movie art collector is to familiarize yourself with the industry. You have already taken a significant step in this direction by reading and studying this reference guide. There are a number of books that have been written over the years about movie posters. Unfortunately, some are no longer in print, but bookstores can sometimes still acquire them. These are a few of the more well-known books on movie posters:

A Separate Cinema, Fifty Years of Black Cast Posters, by John Kisch and Edward Mapp, Noonday Press, New York.
The Disney Poster, by Jim Fanning, Hyperion, New York.
The Movie Poster Book, by Steven Schapiro and David Chierichetti, E.P. Dalton, New York.
Price Guide and Introduction to Movie Posters and Movie Memorabilia, by James Dietz, Jr., Baja Press, San Diego, California.

Reel Art: Great Posters from the Golden Age of the Silver Screen, by Stephen Robello and Richard Allen, Abbeville Press, New York.

Starstruck, the Wonderful World of Movie Memorabilia, by Robert Heide and John Gilman, Doubleday & Company, Garden City, New York.

Research the Current Movie Art Market

As has been explained throughout this reference guide, there are no set prices for movie art. The value of a specific poster is determined by the seller, and the potential buyer has to make a knowledgeable decision as to whether or not the price is fair. Poster prices for the same title can vary significantly between sellers depending on a number of variables. It would behoove potential buyers to do a little research before buying.

The best way to study the movie art market is to see what price collectors, dealers and auction houses are advertising for particular items, and then comparing these figures to actual sale prices. This can be done in a number of ways: subscribing to trade publications, studying price guides, attending movie paper shows, acquiring catalogs from movie poster dealers throughout the country, talking with collectors and dealers, and monitoring auctions.

Trade Publications and Price Guides

There are a number of trade publications, price guides and auction reports that are available to collectors. These publications are extremely valuable tools for monitoring the movie art market.

Big Reel
Antique Trader Publications
P.O. Box 1050
100 Bryant St.
Dubuque, IA 52003
Telephone: (319) 588-2073

Collecting Hollywood
P.O. Box 2512
Chattanooga, TN 37409
Telephone: (615) 265-5515

Movie Collectors World
Arena Publishing, Inc.
P.O. Box 309-T
Fraser, MI 48026
Telephone: (810) 744-4311

Classic Images
P.O. Box 809
Muscatine, IA 52761
Telephone: (319) 263-2331

[Note: *Movie Collectors World* is a major source of information for buying and selling posters. It is an ideal publication for a beginning collector.]

Movie Poster Price Database
Box 114
Hyde Park, NY 12538
Telephone: (918) 452-1998
[Note: We find the *Movie Poster Price Database* publications to be the most useful, particularly when we are looking for price information on a particular poster. Overall, we use these books more often than any of the other publications combined.]

Warren's Movie Poster Price Guide
Jon P. Warren
Harmony Books
New York
[Note: Jon Warren is also the publisher of *Collecting Hollywood.*]

Attend Movie Paper Shows

Movie paper shows are held in many cities throughout the country at various times during the year. They are held quarterly, semi-annually or annually. The dates, times and locations of these shows are normally advertised in one or more of the trade publications listed above.

Movie Poster Dealers and Collectors

Because of the growing popularity of this industry, movie poster dealers have dramatically increased in numbers. There are movie poster dealers located in all major cities or regions of the country. Most of these dealers will regularly advertise in one or more of the trade publications listed above.

Individual collectors also advertise in these trade publications. Be sure to check the "Classified Ad" section which contains names of collections who are buying, selling, trading or looking for specific items.

Names of dealers and collectors can also be obtained by calling a few of those that advertise in these papers. Check your Yellow Pages under the title "Collectibles" or "Posters" for any listings in your area.

Auctions/Auction Houses

Because of the dramatic rise in the value of some movie posters, many prospective sellers are interested in receiving top dollar for their materials. To eliminate the necessity of scouring the country for the highest bid, movie poster auction houses were created. In addition, prestigious art auction houses, such as Sotheby's and Christie's, have added movie posters and other movie related memorabilia to their auction wares. These auctions can be an excellent source for obtaining movie art, particularly rare and sought-after materials.

How Do Auctions Operate? Most auction houses operate on a consignment basis—receiving a percentage of the selling price from both the purchaser and the seller. The auctions can operate in any number of ways. For example, some may hold open auctions while others may take bids by telephone or by mail.

Selling Posters Through Auction Houses: There are some considerations that should be made before submitting a poster to an auction for sale. A would-be seller should check with the auction house to determine the following:

What is the commission that will be paid on the sale?

What is the date of the auction and how soon do you have to submit the poster? (Sometimes the poster can be tied up for six months or more.)

Are there any other charges (besides the commission) that are involved, such as:

Fees for poster appraisal.

Fees for displaying the poster in a catalog (most auction houses charge for the ad, and the prices vary depending on whether the ad is in color or black and white).

Insurance.

Are there any presentation charges?

Can you place a minimum price that you will accept to sell the poster? If the minimum is not met, is there a fee for the "no sale"?

How long does it take to get your money after the poster is sold?

[Note: Unless your poster is extremely rare or valuable, you may actually fare better by selling your poster at a discount rate locally instead of tying it up for as much as four to six months and having to pay all associated expenses.]

Buying Posters Through Auction Houses: Auctions can offer an opportunity to acquire excellent posters at very reasonable rates. However, precautions should also be made before making any purchases. Consider the following:

Is the auction house known and reputable?

Who has appraised the posters? Many auction houses utilize the services of well known and nationally recognized movie poster dealers to establish an appraised market value range for posters.

Most auction catalogs will contain an appraised value range. How does this price compare with auction reports or other such publications (for example, the *Movie Poster Database*)?

Is there a buyer's commission?

Are there associated handling charges (like shipping, insurance, etc.)?

What is the condition of the poster?

Is the poster an original or a rerelease?

What type of guarantee is being offered and how long does it last? Can you return the item if it is sold as an original and you later determine that it is a reissue?

Utilizing Auctions/Auction Houses: Buying and selling movie materials through auction houses can be safe, economical and enjoyable. However, the above precautions should be considered. Please be aware, however, of the potential to get caught up in what is known as "frenzy buying." It is recommended that before bidding on any poster, research be conducted and a price range/budget be set. *Do not exceed the price range you establish.* If there are any questions or doubts, no major purchases or sales should be made without further consultation with a movie poster expert.

Monitoring Auction Houses for Market Values: Monitoring auctions can provide insight into the current value and marketability of certain movie posters. Most major auction houses employ the services of movie poster experts to appraise the market value and condition of posters presented at their auctions. These appraisers will then set a market value range for the poster. Monitoring the market ranges established by these experts can be used as a measuring tool for collectors when assessing the value of their collections.

Please note, however, that the price ranges established by the appraisers is a more accurate measuring tool than the actual auction results. The actual prices paid for posters at auctions can be misleading, as auction results are directly affected by any number of variables. For example, "frenzy buying" and sheer auction competitiveness among buyers has resulted in many posters being sold for prices greatly exceeding their values. Conversely, certain circumstances, such as a poster being placed at the end of the auction program when buyers have already exhausted their budgets, results in many posters being sold for prices well below their market value.

Because of the variables associated with auction purchases, actual auction results should only be considered when viewed over a long period of time and among many auctions. The price ranges that are affixed by the appraising experts for the auctions are much more reliable for assessing market value.

Monitoring auctions are an excellent way to stay abreast of the movie art market in addition to acquiring or selling posters. By acquiring the catalogs or listings from these auctions, a collector can: (1) see what is available on the market; and (2) get an idea of its value based on the estimation of the expert or experts used by the auction. Comparing these to the publications dealing with actual auction results will give a collector a good feel as to what a particular poster or posters is worth on the current market.

The following lists some of the larger auction houses:

Butterfield Auctions
7601 Sunset
Los Angeles, CA 90046
Telephone: (213) 850-7500

Poster Auctions International
37 Riverside Drive
New York, NY 10023
Telephone: (212) 787-4000

Camden House
427 N. Canan Drive
Beverly Hills, CA 92010
Telephone: (310) 246-1212

Reynolds Mill Auction
2 Patrick St.
Waterford, VA 22190
Telephone: (703) 882-3574

Christie's Auction
219 E. 67th Street
New York, NY 10021
Telephone: (212) 606-0400

Sotheby's Auction House
1334 York Avenue
New York, NY 10021
Telephone: (212) 606-7000

Lowery Auctions
3818 W. Magnolia Blvd.
Burbank, CA 91505
Telephone: (818) 972-9080

Superior Auctions
9478 W. Olympic Blvd.
Beverly Hills, CA 90212
Telephone: (310) 203-9855

Odyssey Auctions
510A S. Corona Mall
Corona, CA 91720
Telephone: (909) 371-7137

Vintage Poster Auctions
2044 Euclid Avenue
Cleveland, OH 44115
Telephone: (216) 781-1821

Develop Reputable Sources for Your Materials

Unfortunately, as in every industry, there are a few "dishonest" dealers and collectors. Knowing the market and talking with other collectors can help to weed out the "undesirables." *The rule of thumb should be—check them out before sending cash!* Once you develop one or more reliable sources, it is best to stick with them or ask them about other collectors or dealers. Although the industry covers the globe, the world of movie art is really quite small, and those in the industry are normally quite familiar with the more prominent dealers and collectors.

Learn the Proper Way to Handle
and Store Your Posters

Knowing how and where to acquire movie art is only one side of the equation—the other is learning how to handle and store your posters once you get them.

Regardless of whether you have paid $5 or $5,000 for a poster, it is essential that it be properly cared for, particularly in terms of its value increasing over the years. There are a few reminders which a collector should set to memory:

- **NEVER trim, cut, punch holes or in any way change the size or appearance of a poster** (unless you really don't care if it loses its value as a collectible). The value of a poster significantly decreases if the poster has been altered.
- **NEVER have a poster drymounted if it is going to be framed** (unless you really don't care if it loses its value as a collectible). The dry-mounting process requires that the poster be "glued" to a backing; and the only way it can be removed from the glued backing is by a professional restorer.
- **NEVER use standard cellophane tape and NEVER put tape directly on the front of the poster** to repair small tears in the poster. If you wish to use tape, use acid-free tape that can be purchased from an art supply shop and tape on the back. If a piece of the poster tears off, keep the piece and send it to be professionally restored.
- **NEVER write or mark on your poster, even on the back.** Certain markers can eat right through the posters. Pen and pencil marks can cause see-throughs which detract from the poster's appearance.
- **NEVER place your poster in direct sunlight or under UV lights.**

Shipping Posters

A lot of damage to movie posters can be attributable to handling during shipping, or the lack of care that goes into preparing a poster for shipping. There is not much a collector can do about the individuals who will be handling the package once it leaves their protection. However, a carefully prepared packing can sometimes reduce the chances of shipping damage. Always use thick poster tubes or bubble envelopes for shipping. If you do not have these supplies or cannot get them, then have it sent by a shipping expert.

Storing

Posters can be severely damaged if proper precautions are not taken for storing posters. If the posters are not going to be framed, they should be placed in a plastic bag (if folded) or a tube (if rolled) and placed in a cool, dry climate. Keep the posters away from insects and pests. Never place a poster directly in the sun or under UV lights.

Framing/Mounting

Posters should be mounted/framed by a professional who recognizes the value of the poster as a collectible. **The poster should never be drymounted.** If the poster is going to be in a glass frame, it should have an acid-free backing board and be matted so that the poster does not directly come in contact with the glass.

If a poster is going to be linen-backed, be sure that it is done by a professional who uses the "double-mounting" process. In this process, the poster is first pasted (using a vegetable cellulose paste) to Japanese rice paper and then mounted to linen or duck cloth. Posters should never be mounted "paper to cloth." The friction that is created by the constant rubbing of poster paper against cloth can result in the disintegration of the poster.

Regular Handling

A poster should always be handled delicately. Constant unrolling or unfolding will result in unnecessary wear and tear on the poster. It is best to limit repeated opening and closing of a poster.

Leaving a poster lying around can also create problems. Things can be dropped on it to cause wrinkling; water or other liquids can be spilled; pen marks or other marks accidentally applied, etc. Keep the poster either mounted/framed or properly stored except for limited and careful viewings.

Restoration

Accidents do happen and posters can get damaged to the point of their value being adversely affected. Many of the problems caused by accidents can be repaired, but most should be done by a professional restorer.

Proper professional restoration can restore a poster to its "near mint" or better condition. However, cost considerations need to be made before proceeding to a professional restorer.

The first consideration is whether the poster has some value (be it monetary or sentimental) that would warrant restoration. If the restoration is merely to increase its value, then the costs involved would have to be heavily weighed before beginning. If, on the other hand, the poster has a sentimental value, then the restoration costs may not be so significant, although an estimate is also recommended.

Because movie posters are unique, it is recommended that only properly trained "movie art restorers" be utilized for restoration. There are a number of these "professionals" in the industry. The following is a list of those well known in the movie art industry. Before proceeding to any one of them, however, it is recommended that further research be taken. Talk to other collectors and dealers to get their input into their past dealings with certain restorers. Many of these restorers specialize in certain areas of restoration. In addition, prices and turnaround times may vary, so it is best to do some detective work before narrowing down a prospective restorer.

The following is a list of some of the more recognized names in movie poster restoration:

Crowell Havens Beech
172 Bella Vista Avenue
Belvedere Island, CA 94920
Telephone: (415) 435-1929

Igor Edelman
7466 Beverly Blvd. #205
Los Angeles, CA 90036
Telephone: (213) 934-4219

Roger Fenton
12109 Dewey Street
Los Angeles, CA 90066
Telephone: (310) 391-1078

J. Fields Studio/Gallery
55 West 17th St., 6th Floor
New York, NY 10011
Telephone: (212) 989-4520

Funny Face Productions
320 Riverside
Northhampton, MA 01060
Telephone: (413) 586-0778

Joe Hernandez
701 Seagaze Street
Oceanside, CA 92054
Telephone: (619) 721-5528

Judy Jones
Poster Patch
Fremont, CA
Telephone: (510) 791-8209
(Calls only accepted)

Eric Panelle
1217 E. San Joaquin
Sierra Tulare, CA 93274
Telephone: (209) 686-4006

Jim Sanchez
484 Frederick St., Apt. A
San Francisco, CA 94117
Telephone: (415) 752-0881

Dan Strebin
P.O. Box 312
Santa Monica, CA 90406
Telephone: (310) 314-7036

Don't Get Taken

There is a bond that exists amongst those of us blessed (or should I say cursed) with a collector's spirit. This chapter is our attempt to share with our "brothers and sisters" the lessons that we have learned since beginning our quest for movie posters many years ago. Sounding more like parents than contemporaries, let us pass on a few pearls of wisdom when purchasing movie posters:

LOOK CAREFULLY!
LOOK BEFORE YOU LEAP!
KNOWLEDGE IS POWER!
COLLECTORS BEWARE!

All of these old adages should be committed to the memories of every movie poster collector. The key is knowledge. The more you know, the less chance you will have of being fooled or taken on your acquisition.

Here are a few suggestions that we offer based on our own experiences:

DON'T just take someone's word on the poster you are looking at purchasing. We get calls constantly from dealers who honestly do not know what they have. The movie poster industry is so diverse that *no one can know it all!*

DO inspect any poster before purchasing. Check for things like

- Is it the right size? For example, if it is supposed to be a "one sheet" and it measures 24" × 36", you know it is a commercial poster and not a legitimate one sheet.
- What kind of paper is it printed on? If it is 14" × 36" and printed on thin paper when it should be on card stock, it might be foreign instead of American.
- Feel the paper. Older posters were printed on a cheap paper stock and feel similar to cheap newspaper. In the 1970s, clay coating was introduced on posters. The posters with the clay coating are smooth. Glossy paper came into existence in the 1980s, so posters from this

time period should have a glossy shine—a poster from the 1950s should not!

- One sheets were sent to the film exhibitors and theatres folded until the late 1970s. From this period, more and more posters were sent in rolled condition. If, however, you come across a poster from the 1960s or earlier which has never been folded, you had better ask some more questions.
- Check the borders. Are they even or do they appear to be trimmed? Measure for balance. Look for any writing in the borders, such as the name of printing companies. Does it say "printed in the U.S.A."?
- Check the fine print. Many foreign posters have all the names in English, but some of the fine print is in the native language of the country. Look for any "unusual" spellings.
- Hold the poster up, preferably with light behind it. Imperfections in the poster will show. Tape, marks, bleedthroughs, tears, and holes are more easily overlooked when the poster is lying down or has something behind it to help hide the light. (Some dealers display their posters on white boards because it helps to hide the holes and imperfections.) Black backgrounds help to hide bleedthroughs.
- Look at the back side of the poster. If repairs have been made to a poster, they will show up better on the back side.
- Never purchase a poster that is framed and matted without first removing the frame and looking at the back.

New Technology Is Creating New Opportunities for Fakes

With the advancement of printing processes, computers and color reproduction, the area of fakes is one of growing concern among collectors. The phrase "Buyer Beware" should be changed to "Collector Beware," as more movie buffs join the ranks of collectors. Unfortunately, more individuals with the ability to produce fakes and forgeries are preying on unsuspecting novice collectors.

With the growing number of incidents in an area that will almost certainly grow, we would like to present several specific examples where we have personal experience dealing with some of these problem areas:

Revenge of the Jedi: We have been asked at least a thousand times: What about the *Return of the Jedi* poster. As mentioned earlier, two different *Revenge of the Jedi* posters (one dated on the bottom and one without a date) were issued by the movie studio and then recalled when the name of the film was changed to *Return of the Jedi*. A mad scramble ensued among collectors to snatch up these posters before they were recalled by the studios. These posters became instantly sought-after, and their price skyrocketed. With the prices going through the roof, three different fakes suddenly appeared on the market. The most common of those was a lot of 2,000 reproduced in Japan. These reproductions were so good that they easily passed for originals. Many dealers became so frustrated that they stopped handling them altogether and the price plummeted. With the number of fakes still on the market, the poster has not been able to regain its value.

There is one way to recognize the difference between this well-made fake and the real McCoy. Looking at the bottom right hand corner of the artwork, there is a little "cloud" in the corner. With clouds all around the artwork, this particular cloud looks like it belongs. However, on the original one sheet, the right hand corner is solid black.

And while we are discussing *Star Wars*...

In 1992, *Star Wars* Style "D" was reissued. This poster is identical to the original in artwork. The original copyright year is on the reissue, but there is no "R" in the bottom border to indicate that it is a reissue. If you have two versions to compare, you will notice that the reissue is on a slightly glossier paper. If you can't compare, please note the style indication. The style notation on the original issue is: Style 'D'. The 1992 reissue does not have the single quote marks or tick marks (' ') around the letter "D." It is listed simply as Style D. The reissue also has a computer number listed above the "D" which is not on the original version.

The *Blues Brothers* Poster: The majority of the *Blues Brothers* posters that we have received in the past year or so have been fakes. When looking at the poster you see what appears to be a tear across the bottom. However, when

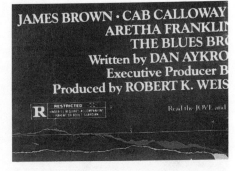

Left: Blues Brothers fake. Notice the "tears" on bottom. *Right:* Closeup of tears shows up, but it is a *picture* of tears—the poster is not torn.

you "feel" the poster, you discover that the "tear" is not there. It is a picture of a tear. When this poster was reproduced, the counterfeiters apparently did not have access to a poster in mint or even near mint condition, and simply reproduced the poster, tears and all.

On the "white style" *Blues Brothers* poster (not shown), there are two lines of credit information on the bottom. A careful look will show that the bottoms of letters that normally fall below the print line have been "chopped off" during the reproduction.

Dawn of the Dead **Poster:** This poster is a cult favorite with many collectors. A copy of this poster was purchased at a sci-fi convention. It was autographed by the film's director, David Argento, who was attending the convention. When the poster was sent to me by a friend, I asked him why he had a "fake" poster autographed. He literally flew into a rage because he had purchased several copies.

This poster is in rolled, mint condition. However, it is quite obviously a reproduction. If you look at the picture, you will see fold lines where the poster was "folded." However, this particular poster has never been folded. What is seen on the poster are fold lines that have been "copied" onto the poster.

Beautiful fake of *Dawn of the Dead*, autographed by assistant director Dario Argento.

A Hard Day's Night: Quite a few fake *A Hard Day's Night* lobby cards have cropped up around the country. The lobby cards have great color and are on a decent grade card stock. However, you will notice on the photograph there are "staple hole marks" in the corners of the lobby cards. A physical investigation, however, reveals that there were never any staples in the card. These are merely "pictures" of staple holes—the staples that were on the original lobby card. Reproductions of the one sheet for this title also exist, and are so well done that only the type of paper it is printed on gives it away as a fake.

James Bond Dilemma: Counterfeits on James Bond materials are fairly common, especially on the earlier titles like *Dr. No* because of their simple artwork. We have been told that some

Beautiful fake of *A Hard Day's Night* but can be spotted by a couple of staple holes in the corners that show as black dots on the fake.

counterfeits are so good that the only clue that they are fakes is the missing NSS rubber stamp on the back. To solve the problem, some counterfeiters just linen-back the posters.

Another problem with Bond materials is that in the early 1980s, the studio rereleased a series of Bond posters, but didn't mark them as rereleases. The only way to tell that they are rereleases is by the glossier paper that they were printed on. We haven't come across all of them yet, but we have run into several different versions.

A Group of Oldies to Look Out For: There are some *various* size older posters like the *Thin Man* that you may find around. Be sure to look at the bottom border to see if it says, "Po-Flake of Normal II 61761." You should always:

1. Beware of printers' names on the bottom of any poster. (This is not to be confused with the names of "lithographers" which are commonly found on the bottom of legitimate theatre posters.)
2. Beware of any type of zip code being listed on a poster that pre-dates the 1960s. Zip codes were not introduced until then.
3. Beware of posters that are "real cheap" or "bargains," because they may be commercial.

If you are a "B" western fanatic, here's one for you to think about. Posters for westerns from the 1930s and 1940s were not dated. Some studios (especially Republic) would rerelease their movies a few years later and reissue the original movie poster. Unfortunately, these reissued posters were not marked as such, so they are very hard to distinguish from original issues.

For example, Gene Autry made a number of movies in the 1930s. When he went into the U.S. Army, Republic rereleased many of his early movies and reissued the original movie posters. Because they are not dated, it is very difficult to tell the difference between the original and reissue posters. The only way to distinguish the two is the Republic logo, which changed between the time the original and the reissue were released.

Consider the movie poster for *Yodelin' Kid from Pine Ridge*. When this movie was originally released in the early 1930s, the Republic logo consisted of a coat of arms crest. In November of 1936, Republic changed their logo to the capitol dome. It was later changed to an eagle. In this case, the poster is obviously a reissue because when this film was originally released, Republic's logo was a coat of arms crest (and should have been such on the poster).

So, if you know when a movie was originally released, and the poster has a logo that was not used at that particular time, then you can assume it is a reissue. Confusing, huh?

Another area of concern involves a recent trend in which movie studios send out movie posters to independent advertising agencies, who in turn send people out, mostly at night, to tack them up on walls around a community. The *What's Love Got to Do with It* poster is an example. Before the movie studios send these posters to the ad agencies, they sometimes bore a quarter-sized hole through them so they will not get confused with the posters sent to the theatres.

A few other miscellaneous tidbits:

TV posters are gaining some limited acceptance with some collectors and dealers. These are posters that are issued for television shows, usually just before the new season. This is not legitimate theatre art—just another situation that is becoming more common in movie art collecting, and may even be included in dealers' catalogs because they are gaining in popularity.

Lastly, there are a few dealers in New York and California that are intentionally selling unmarked reissued posters as originals, under the advertising language of "authentic movie posters." They are *authentic*—they are just not originals!

In this chapter, we have focused heavily on some of the "negative" sides of this industry. Please understand that the positives far outweigh the negatives. We merely wanted to cover some of the areas that can present problems, particularly for new collectors. On the positive side, we have met a lot of great people who share in our enthusiasm and who are trying to help others understand and enjoy this hobby. For example, the *Star Wars Poster of Posters* was the

This 1985 Kilian Enterprises release, with a writeup on the back of each poster, has been a tremendous help to *Star Wars* collectors.

brainchild of Jeff Kilian, and has proven itself a tremendous help to *Star Wars* poster collectors.

Let us assure you that this is an extremely enjoyable hobby—it has given us much pleasure for many years. For all the problems we have encountered, we have also had a tremendous amount of fun—hunting, finding, framing, and talking about our acquisitions.

Our best advice to any collector, but particularly a new one, is to learn about the industry and to try to find other collectors who share your areas of interest to talk to, learn from, or trade with.

There are a lot of good materials still on the market at reasonable prices— but this is not going to last long. As the number of collectors grows, these materials will be snatched up and then watch the prices rise.

HAPPY COLLECTING!

Bibliography

Bardeche, Maurice, and Robert Brasillach. *The History of Motion Pictures.* New York: W.W. Norton and The Museum of Modern Art, 1938.

Dietz, James S., Jr. *Price Guide and Introduction to Movie Posters and Movie Memorabilia.* San Diego California: Baja Press, 1982.

Heide, Robert, and John Gilman. *Starstruck, the Wonderful World of Movie Memorabilia.* Garden City, New York: Doubleday & Company, 1986.

Robello, Stephen, and Richard Allen. *Reel Art: Great Posters from the Golden Age of the Silver Screen.* New York: Abbeville Press, 1988.

Schapiro, Steve, and David Chierichetti. *The Movie Poster Book.* New York: E.P. Dalton, 1979.

Weiss, Ken, and Ed Goodgold. *To Be Continued....* New York: Crown Publishers, 1972.

Index